Primary Atlas Activity Book

Mapwise

2

Rita Doyle and Catherine Hynes

5th Class & 6th Class

The Educational Company of Ireland

Foreword

Written by experienced primary school teachers, *Mapwise* is a series of geography activity books intended for pupils at third to sixth class level. This exciting new series will encourage children to work as active geographers, developing a thorough understanding and appreciation of their local and wider environment.

Mapwise follows the specific content and skills outlined in the Geography Curriculum, and incorporates the prescribed strands and strand units for each class level. The series offers a comprehensive range of maps and assignments which explore the physical geography of Europe, America, Asia and the wider world. It can be used in conjunction with any atlas. Innovative activities and challenging research projects will enable children to develop vital map, globe and graphical skills, together with essential geographical investigation skills.

A comprehensive range of information is presented using a variety of high-interest formats. These include attractive photographs, colourful illustrations and high-quality maps. Many of these features will serve as stimuli for discussion-based activities – reflecting the centrality of oral language in the curriculum.

The series also incorporates high-interest 'More About Maps!' information segments, and fact-based 'Guess What?' panels.

Mapwise is supported by a range of useful ICT resources. A detailed online teacher's resource pack accompanies the series. This includes the answers to each exercise. Other online resources include a wide variety of printable activity sheets, templates on each topic and suggestions for additional extension activities. These supplementary online resources are designed to assist the teacher in the delivery of the lesson, and to reinforce the work undertaken in each topic area. To access these ICT resources, teachers will need to register at **www.edcodigital.ie**.

Recent curriculum reports and evaluations have suggested that the development of a range of teaching approaches and strategies, such as active learning, differentiation, integration and assessment, is central to effective teaching and learning. In line with this recommendation, *Mapwise* incorporates a wide range of suitable teaching methodologies. Children are encouraged to undertake a variety of individual, pair and group-work research activities.

Moreover, the structure of each *Mapwise* topic reflects the finding that assessment and differentiation are the core foundations of teaching and learning. Each chapter includes a carefully differentiated range of higher-order and fun activities. These high-interest activities have been structured so that children at all levels will experience both challenge and success. Online quiz sheets, comprehensive revision exercises and printable blank maps will enable teachers to generate accurate assessment profiles for each child. Finally, opportunities for integration with other curricular areas and linkage within subjects have been highlighted throughout the text.

We hope that children and teachers alike will enjoy exploring the world through *Mapwise*!

Rita Doyle and Catherine Hynes

Contents

Ireland

County Towns

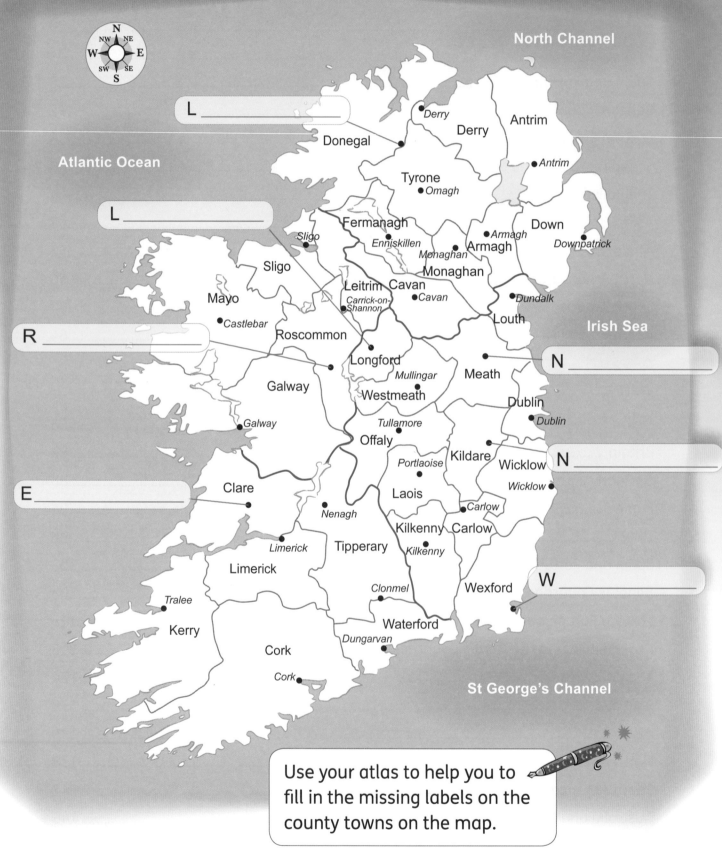

North Channel

Atlantic Ocean

Irish Sea

St George's Channel

L _____

L _____

R _____

E _____

N _____

N _____

W _____

Donegal
Derry
Derry
Antrim
Antrim
Tyrone
Omagh
Fermanagh
Down
Sligo
Enniskillen
Armagh
Armagh
Downpatrick
Sligo
Monaghan
Mayo
Leitrim
Cavan
Monaghan
Castlebar
Carrick-on-Shannon
Cavan
Dundalk
Roscommon
Louth
Longford
Longford
Meath
Galway
Mullingar
Westmeath
Dublin
Galway
Tullamore
Dublin
Offaly
Clare
Kildare
Wicklow
Portlaoise
Laois
Wicklow
Nenagh
Carlow
Kilkenny
Carlow
Limerick
Tipperary
Kilkenny
Limerick
Kilkenny
Tralee
Clonmel
Wexford
Kerry
Waterford
Cork
Dungarvan
Cork

Use your atlas to help you to fill in the missing labels on the county towns on the map.

2

More about Maps!

A county town is the administrative centre of a county. It is usually the biggest town in the county. Use the map to help you to identify three county towns in your province.

Guess What?

The word Navan is a palindrome – you can read it forwards or backwards! Can you think of any other palindromes?

Exercise A

Answer these questions:

1 Which province has the greatest number of counties?

_____

2 List the counties in Munster.

_____

_____

3 What is the largest county in Ireland?

_____

4 Name an inland county in Connacht.

_____

5 Name the largest inland county in Ireland.

_____

6 What county is southwest of Laois?

_____

7 List two cities in Ulster.

  (a) _____

  (b) _____

8 Name a maritime county in Leinster.

_____

Exercise B

Wordsearch

Find the names of the towns hidden in this wordsearch. In the box provided, list the county where each town can be found. Use your atlas to help you.

```
V J O Y W O H I D Y I A S E Y L R T E L T M Z O B
F V U U O G D R O S C O M M O N K E N N I S O S E
W M E R E V L I N T A L L A G H T I O R T Y Z S F
I Z M Q A L I X W X Q Z V R H U Q W M J C O I G V
C T U E O P M N K Y A O D U N G A R V A N O R N P
K R Y Q Z Q E O M M M U L L I N G A R N A A R Z B
L I F L G Q R I U R Y V V D C G H L T L B E M O I
O M C A R R I C K O N S H A N N O N T E R G W N C
W H L J P I C L A C G M S D U F P R L O D A C R N
J S M P N B K H G R Z K B W S A O T M N U A G Q T
L L O N G F O R D U L Q I N D P S A G M F T B K C
V P J C A N E N A G H O A G E A L D U N D A L K L
M W S M S V B Z F U K V W I C L H D U B L I N P S
G Q Q C C C A W P W A L S R U D D R T R A L E E O
F U R U W X C N L C U M A T E H C G Z A G L H D E
```

TOWN	COUNTY	TOWN	COUNTY
Carlow		Mullingar	
Carrick-on-Shannon		Navan	
Castlebar		Nenagh	
Cavan		Portlaoise	
Dublin		Roscommon	
Dundalk		Tallaght	
Dungarvan		Tralee	
Ennis		Trim	
Limerick		Tullamore	
Longford		Wicklow	

Map that Route!

The under-twelve hurling team from Tralee, Co. Kerry, has reached the All-Ireland final in Croke Park this summer. Using a blue coloured pencil and a ruler, mark the towns that the team will travel through to get from Tralee to Dublin.

The team would like to take a coastal route home from Dublin to Tralee. Using a ruler and a green coloured pencil, mark the towns that the team will travel through.

Write a paragraph about one of the towns that the team will pass through on the route home.

Town: _____

_____

_____

_____

_____

_____

_____

_____

_____

_____

_____

_____

_____

_____

_____

_____

_____

Rivers, Lakes, Bays, Headlands and Islands

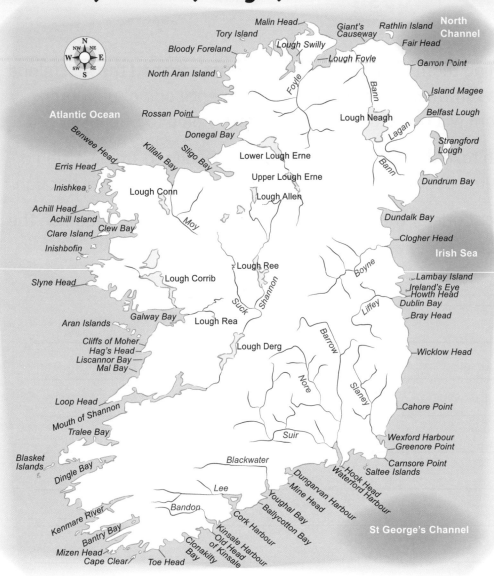

Mark the peninsulas in Munster using a red **X**.

Circle the Aran Islands (off the Galway coast), using brown and the Blasket Islands, using green.

Mark the most northerly point in Ireland, using a blue circle.

Use your map and atlas to help you to complete the grid.

Headland	County
Fair Head	
Mizen Head	
Hook Head	
Howth Head	
Malin Head	

Island(s)	County
Blasket Islands	
Aran Islands	
Tory Island	
Achill Island	
Lambay Island	

More about Maps!

A **peninsula** is a long piece of land that juts out into the sea. It is surrounded by water on three sides.

A **bay** is a wide, curved opening along the coastline. It is usually surrounded by land on three sides.

A **headland** is a high area of hard rock that juts out into the sea. It is surrounded by water on three sides.

Our coastlines are constantly changing shape. Look at the map and compare the east and west coasts of Ireland. What differences do you note? What has caused this?

Guess What?

Lambay Island is the largest island off the coast of Co. Dublin. This was the scene of the first Viking raid on Ireland in AD795.

The Vikings used the River Liffey to move goods throughout the city. The river still plays an important role in the city's trade.

Exercise A

Answer these questions:

1 List two rivers that flow into the Irish Sea.

(a) _____

(b) _____

2 In which direction does the River Shannon flow? _____

3 Name the river that flows into the Atlantic Ocean at Killala Bay.

_____

4 Name the river that flows into the sea at Belfast Lough.

_____

5 Name the lough on the north coast, to the east of Lough Swilly.

_____

6 Where is the most northerly point in Ireland? _____

7 Name three islands between Mizen Head in the southwest and Erris Head in the west.

(a) _____

(b) _____

(c) _____

8 Name the islands off the coast of Co. Kerry.

_____

9 What is a headland? _____

List two headlands that jut into the Irish Sea.

(a) _____

(b) _____

Guess What?

The Battle of the Boyne took place in 1690.

The Aran Islands are located at the mouth of Galway Bay. They include Inis Mór, Inis Meáin and Inis Oírr.

The Blasket Islands lie off the Dingle Peninsula. Life on these islands was very difficult and the Great Blasket Island was eventually abandoned in 1953.

The Aran Islands, Co. Galway

Exercise B

Use your atlas to help you to list the rivers associated with these towns and cities.

Towns and cities	Rivers
Drogheda	
Athlone	
Kinsale	
Cork	
Belfast	
Derry	
Ballina	
Sligo	
Kilkenny	
Bandon	
Waterford	
Ennis	

Exercise C

Research Time

Prepare a short research project on the Blaskets and present your findings to your class. Arrange your information using these headings:

1 History

2 Flora and Fauna

3 Way of life

4 Culture

5 Evacuation of the islands

The Blasket Islands, Co. Kerry

Mountains

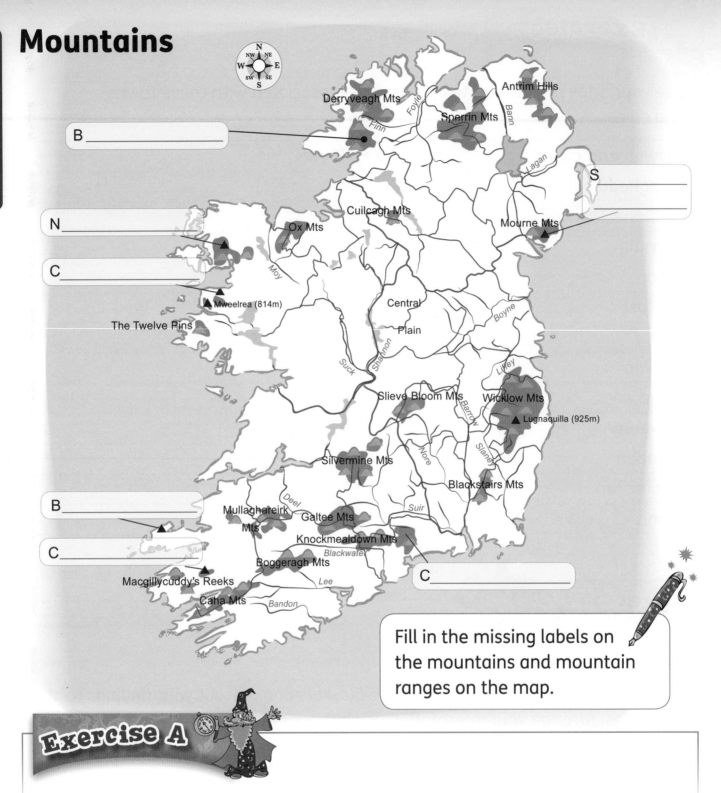

B _____

N _____

C _____

Derryveagh Mts

Finn

Foyle

Sperrin Mts

Antrim Hills

Bann

Lagan

S _____

Cuilcagh Mts

Ox Mts

Mourne Mts

Moy

▲ Mweelrea (814m)

The Twelve Pins

Central

Plain

Boyne

Suck

Shannon

Liffey

Slieve Bloom Mts

Wicklow Mts

Barrow

▲ Lugnaquilla (925m)

Silvermine Mts

Nore

Slaney

Blackstairs Mts

B _____

Deel

Mullaghareirk
Mts

Galtee Mts

Suir

C _____

Knockmealdown Mts

Blackwater

Boggeragh Mts

Lee

C _____

Macgillycuddy's Reeks

Caha Mts

Bandon

Fill in the missing labels on the mountains and mountain ranges on the map.

Exercise A

Answer these questions:

1 What is the name given to the area in the centre of Ireland?

_____

2 Name three mountain ranges in Connacht.

(a) _____

(b) _____

(c) _____

3 In what counties are the Galtee Mountains? _____

4 What is the source of a river? Where is it usually found? _____

_____

_____

5 Where is the source of the River Lagan? _____

6 Where is the highest mountain in Ireland? _____

_____

Exercise B

Draw a bar graph in your copy to represent the approximate height of the mountains listed below:

- Carrauntoohil: 1,000m
- Croagh Patrick: 750m
- Mount Brandon: 950m
- Lugnaquilla: 900m
- Sperrin Mountains: 650m
- Comeragh Mountains: 800m
- Slieve Donard: 850m
- Blackstairs Mountains: 800m

1 Name the highest mountain. _____

2 Name the lowest mountain range. _____

3 What is the average height of these mountains? _____

Exercise C

Down to Business

Working with your class, choose a major mountain range in Ireland. In pairs, create a plan for an activity centre to be located in this area. Who will your centre cater for? What facilities will be on offer? What will your centre be called? State why you are choosing this location.

Present your findings to the class. Hold a class vote to see which project the class thinks is most suitable.

Britain:
England, Scotland and Wales

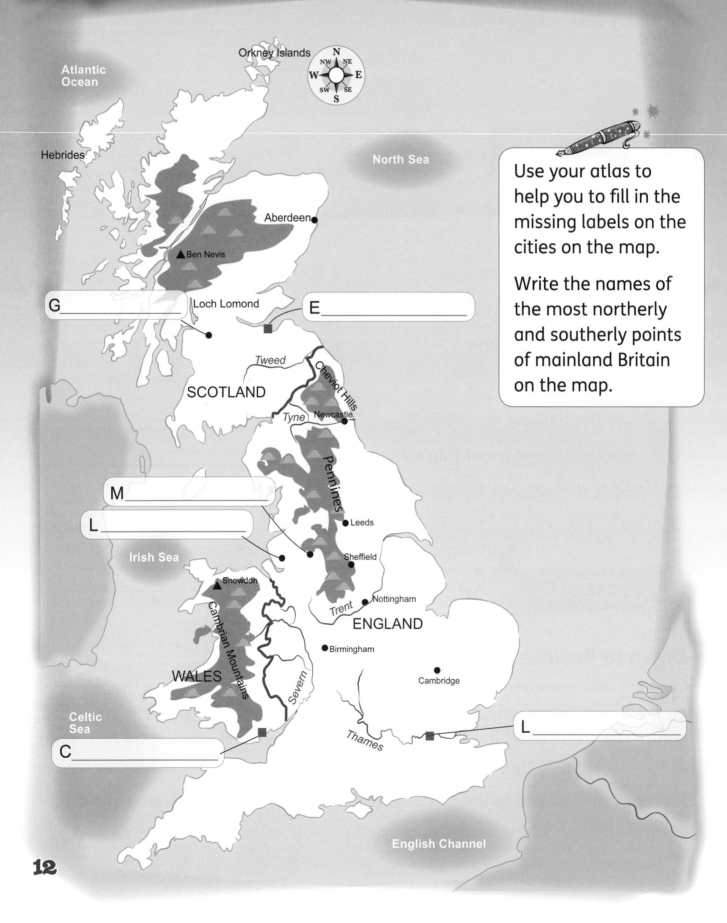

Orkney Islands

Atlantic Ocean

Hebrides

North Sea

Aberdeen

▲ Ben Nevis

G_____

Loch Lomond

E_____

Tweed

Cheviot Hills

SCOTLAND

Tyne   Newcastle

Pennines

M_____

L_____

Irish Sea

Leeds

Sheffield

▲ Snowdon

Cambrian Mountains

Trent   Nottingham

ENGLAND

Birmingham

WALES

Severn

Cambridge

Celtic Sea

C_____

Thames

L_____

English Channel

Use your atlas to help you to fill in the missing labels on the cities on the map.

Write the names of the most northerly and southerly points of mainland Britain on the map.

More about Maps!

Land's End is the most westerly point in England. Many tourists travel there to see the magnificent views of the Atlantic Ocean. John O'Groats is a village which is close to the most northerly point of mainland Britain.

The white cliffs of Dover are located on the southeast coast of England. They are made of chalk and are constantly eroded by the sea, keeping them a bright white colour. On a clear day, the cliffs can be seen easily from France.

The Cheviot Hills are a range of rolling hills between England and Scotland. National parks occupy most of the hills. The North Tyne and tributaries of the River Tweed rise here.

Guess What?

Britain is a monarchy. It has a royal family, whose main house is Buckingham Palace. Although Queen Elizabeth is not responsible for governing the country, she is Head of State.

Exercise A

Answer these questions:

1 Where is the mouth of the River Trent? _____

2 Where is the mouth of the River Tweed? _____

3 List the islands off the northwest coast of Scotland. _____

_____

4 Where are the Orkney Islands located? _____

5 Describe the course of the River Severn. _____

_____

6 Where is the highest peak in Britain? _____

7 Name a major mountain range in Wales. _____

8 Name a major lake in Scotland. _____

9 Where is the highest peak in Wales? _____

10 Choose one of the countries that make up Britain. Write three facts about it.

(a) _____

(b) _____

(c) _____

Guess What?

Each country in Britain has its own patron saint and national emblem:

- The national flower of England is the rose. St George is the patron saint of England.

- The national flower of Scotland is the thistle, a prickly-leaved purple flower. St Andrew is the patron saint of Scotland.

- St David is the patron saint of Wales. The national flower of Wales is the daffodil, which is traditionally worn on St David's Day. Leeks are also considered to be the traditional emblem of Wales!

Exercise B

Make up questions for these answers:

1 _____ ?

This mountain range is commonly referred to as the backbone of England.

2 _____ ?

The tourist attractions here include Tower Bridge, Buckingham Palace and Big Ben.

3 _____ ?

This high mountain is found in Scotland.

4 _____ ?

They are white cliffs that face France.

5 _____ **?**

It is the most westerly point in England.

6 _____ **?**

It is a village beside the most northerly point of Britain.

Exercise C

London Calling!

London lies in the southeast of England, on the River Thames. It is the biggest city in Europe and attracts large numbers of visitors and tourists every year.

A family of four will be spending a weekend in London this summer. There are two parents, an 11-year-old girl, and an 8-year-old boy. Investigate some of the tourist attractions that they could go to see, and identify which ones would best suit this group. Plan each day carefully, identifying the sights that you think they should visit. Design a travel brochure for the family – do not forget to include their itinerary!

Germany

North Sea

DENMARK

Baltic Sea

GERMANY

POLAND

NETHERLANDS

BELGIUM

LUXEMBOURG

CZECH REPUBLIC

FRANCE

Use the Word Box to help you to fill in the missing labels on the map.

AUSTRIA

SWITZERLAND

Bavarian Alps   **Harz Mountains**   **Ore Mountains**

Black Forest   **Rhine**   **Elbe**   **Main**

Danube   **Berlin**   **Düsseldorf**   **Hamburg**   **Bonn**

Munich   **Cologne**   **Frankfurt**   **Zugspitze**

More about Maps!

Germany's major rivers are the Danube, the Elbe, the Oder, the Weser and the Rhine.

Berlin is located in northeast Germany. It is the capital and the largest city in Germany.

Hamburg is Germany's second largest city. It is located on the Elbe River, close to its mouth in the North Sea. Hamburg is the busiest port in Germany.

Guess What?

After World War II, Berlin was divided by the Berlin Wall. In 1989, much of the wall was torn down and the city was reunited.

Exercise A

Answer these questions:

1 What is the capital of Germany? _____

2 What is the highest peak in Germany? _____

3 Name a major mountain range in southern Germany.

_____

4 List the countries that share a land border with Germany.

_____

_____

5 Name a major city in the south of Germany.

_____

6 List the seas that touch Germany. _____

_____

7 Where is the source of the Danube? _____

Exercise B

Complete this crossword:

Across

3 The _ _ _ _ _ Forest is a popular tourist region to the southwest of Germany.

4 This major mountain range lies near Germany's border with the Czech Republic.

6 This popular tourist destination is the capital of Germany.

9 The _ _ _ _ _ _ _ _ Alps are a major mountain range that stretch along the Austrian border.

10 This currency is used in Germany.

11 The highest peak in Germany. It is part of the Bavarian Alps.

The Danube River

Down

1 This is the major language spoken in Germany.

2 The D _ _ _ _ _ is one of the longest rivers in Europe.

5 City along the course of the River Rhine.

7 The River Main flows through this city.

8 This _ _ _ _ divided Berlin into East and West Berlin.

Write the correct name under each photograph. Use the Word Box to help you. Discuss each picture.

River Danube	Berlin Wall	Black Forest
Reichstag	Lake Constance	Cologne Cathedral

Exercise C

Design It

Choose a city in Germany. Design a poster encouraging people to visit it. What slogan will you use? Remember to list the major attractions. What images will you include?

Guess What?

Germany's location at the heart of central Europe has shaped its history. The enormous loss of life in World War I and World War II encouraged Germans to seek a lasting peace in Europe. In 1957, Germany became one of the founding members of the European Community.

France

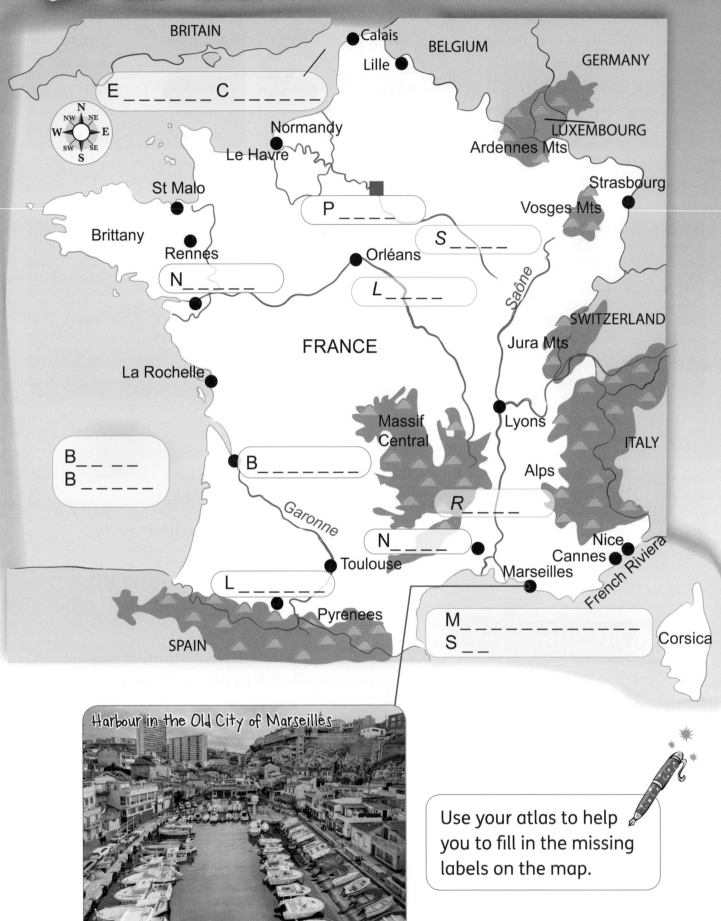

BRITAIN

Calais

BELGIUM

GERMANY

Lille

E _ _ _ _ _ _ _ C _ _ _ _ _ _

N
NW   NE
W   E
SW   SE
S

LUXEMBOURG

Normandy

Ardennes Mts

Le Havre

Strasbourg

St Malo

Vosges Mts

P _ _ _ _ _

Brittany

S _ _ _ _ _

Rennes

Saône

Orléans

N _ _ _ _ _ _

L _ _ _ _

SWITZERLAND

FRANCE

Jura Mts

La Rochelle

Massif
Central

Lyons

ITALY

B _ _ _ _

B _ _ _ _ _

B _ _ _ _ _ _ _ _

Alps

R _ _ _ _ _

Garonne

N _ _ _ _ _

Nice

Cannes

Toulouse

Marseilles

French Riviera

L _ _ _ _ _ _ _

Pyrenees

M _ _ _ _ _ _ _ _ _ _ _ _ _ _ _

Corsica

SPAIN

S _ _

Harbour in the Old City of Marseilles

Use your atlas to help
you to fill in the missing
labels on the map.

20

More about Maps!

Tourism is a very important industry in France. Brittany, Normandy and the French Riviera are among the most popular tourist destinations in the country.

Brittany is a scenic region in northwestern France. It is a peninsula that lies between the English Channel and the Bay of Biscay.

The French Riviera is a narrow coastal strip between the Alps and the Mediterranean. It is famous for its beaches, fashionable resorts and Mediterranean climate.

Exercise A

Answer these questions:

1 List the countries that border France.

_____

_____

_____

_____

_____

_____

Guess What?

Many of the buildings in Normandy date from Norman times and have distinctive wooden beams and whitewashed walls.

The ancient Bayeux Tapestry can be seen in Normandy. This tells the story of the Norman conquest of England by William the Conqueror in 1066.

2 Name the mountain range that forms part of the natural border between France and Spain. _____

3 What is the longest river in France? _____

4 What river flows through Paris? _____

5 Name a popular tourist attraction in France. Write one fact about it.

_____

_____

21

Exercise B

Write the words in blue under the correct photograph.
Discuss each picture.

1 The city of **La Rochelle** is one of the main sea ports in France.

2 An international film festival is held in **Cannes** each spring.

3 Many of the buildings in **Toulouse** are built from an unusual pink stone, giving the city the nickname of *la ville rose*.

4 Many tourists travel along the **River Seine** on open boats known as *bateaux mouches*.

5 The **Bay of Biscay** is noted for its unpredictable weather and its strong currents.

6 Heavy fighting took place in France during **World War I**.

Exercise C

Bon Voyage!

A family has travelled to France using the Channel Tunnel. They have brought their car with them. They intend to drive to the coastal town of St Malo for a short break. After that, they will continue in an easterly direction to spend a few days enjoying the many attractions in France's capital city. Their next destination is Orléans. They will then drive west along the Loire Valley. After a short stay in Nantes, they plan to head south to Bordeaux and to spend two days in a place of pilgrimage in France. They would also like to see the tallest bridge in the world and to spend some time in Lyons. Their final night will be spent in Le Havre and their ferry will depart from this point.

Mark on the map the route that the family will take.

Imagine you are on this family holiday. Write your diary entry after one day of the trip.

Lourdes

Italy

SWITZERLAND

A _ _ _ _

AUSTRIA

SLOVENIA

Milan

V _ _ _ _ _ _ _

Trieste

T _ _ _ _ _

P _

Genoa

ITALY

FRANCE

Florence

A _ _

P _ _ _ _

Arno

A _ _ _ _ _ _ _ _ _
S _ _

Corsica

T _ _ _ _ _ _

M _

N
NW   NE
W   E
SW   SE
S

R _ _ _ _

N _ _ _ _ _ _

S _ _ _ _ _ _ _ _

Tyrrhenian Sea

Capri

Mount Vesuvius

Cagliari

M _ _ _ _ _ _ _ _ _ _ _ _ _ _ _ _ _
S _ _

Palermo

S _ _ _ _ _ _

Mount Etna

Use your atlas to help you to fill in the missing labels on the map.

More about Maps!

Sicily is the largest island in the Mediterranean Sea. Its beautiful beaches and fascinating history make it a popular tourist destination.

Guess What?

Mount Vesuvius is an active volcano in southern Italy, towering high over the Bay of Naples. It erupted on 24 August in AD79, burying the nearby towns and cities in a deep blanket of ash.

Pompeii was an ancient Roman city, buried by the volcanic eruption of Mount Vesuvius. Archaeologists later uncovered the city to find the ruins of many buildings and artefacts.

Exercise A

Answer these questions:

1 What is the capital of Italy? _____

2 What is the principal language of Italy? _____

3 Name two major mountain ranges in Italy.

   (a) _____

   (b) _____

4 Name the two seas that border Italy to the west.

   (a) _____

   (b) _____

5 Where is the mouth of the River Po? _____

6 Name an active volcano on the island of Sicily. _____

7 Name an inland country that borders Italy to the northeast.

   _____

8 Choose one of the following areas: Vatican City, Sardinia, Sicily. In your copy, write five facts that you have learned about the area you selected.

Exercise B

Write questions for the following answers:

1 _____

_____ ?

They are the Apennine Mountains.

2 _____ ?

It is the largest active volcano in Europe.

3 _____ ?

People stay because the volcanic ash is an excellent fertiliser.

4 _____ ?

It is one of the most important tourist destinations in the world. In the old centre, canals are used instead of roads. Many tourists love to take relaxing gondola rides here.

5 _____ ?

They include St Peter's Square, St Peter's Basilica and the Sistine Chapel.

6 _____ ?

They are France, Switzerland, Austria and Slovenia.

Can you name this city in Italy?

Write the correct name under each photograph. Use the Word Box to help you. Discuss each picture.

Sistine Chapel   **Leaning Tower of Pisa**   **Alps**

Sardinia   **Mount Etna**   **Pompeii**

Exercise C

Research Time

Although Mount Etna is Europe's most active volcano, many local people still live and work on its slopes. They refer to it as *il gigante buono* – 'the good giant'. Research the advantages and disadvantages of living on the slopes of an active volcano.

Spain and Portugal

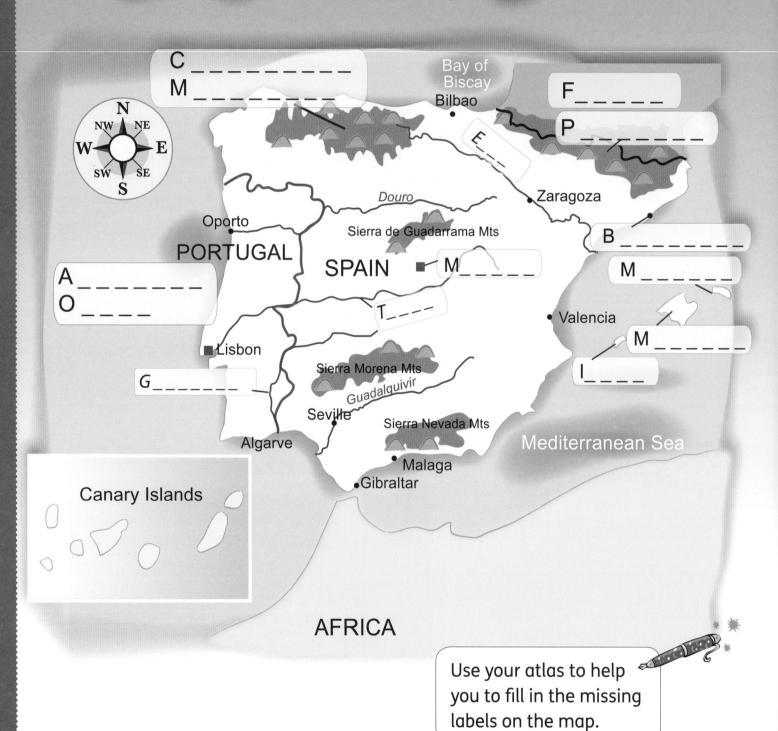

C _ _ _ _ _ _ _ _ _ _
M _ _ _ _ _ _ _ _ _ _

Bay of Biscay
Bilbao

F _ _ _ _ _ _
P _ _ _ _ _ _ _ _ _

N NE
NW
W   E
SW SE
S

E _ _ _ _

Douro

Zaragoza

Oporto

Sierra de Guadarrama Mts

B _ _ _ _ _ _ _ _ _

PORTUGAL

SPAIN   M _ _ _ _ _ _

M _ _ _ _ _ _ _

A _ _ _ _ _ _ _ _ _ _
O _ _ _ _ _

T _ _ _ _

Valencia

M _ _ _ _ _ _ _

Lisbon

Sierra Morena Mts

I _ _ _ _

G _ _ _ _ _ _ _ _

Guadalquivir

Seville

Sierra Nevada Mts

Algarve

Mediterranean Sea

Malaga
Gibraltar

Canary Islands

AFRICA

Use your atlas to help you to fill in the missing labels on the map.

More about Maps!

The Iberian Peninsula is found in southwest Europe. It is separated from the rest of the continent by the Pyrenees Mountains. It includes the countries of Spain and Portugal.

The Canary Islands are a group of mountainous islands in the Atlantic Ocean. They are located about 100 kilometres off the coast of northwest Africa. They belong to Spain.

The Strait of Gibraltar lies between southern Spain and northern Africa. It connects the Atlantic Ocean and the Mediterranean Sea.

Exercise A

Guess What?

Bullfighting is a national sport and popular tourist attraction throughout Spain. Bullfights take place in large outdoor arenas. The aim is for one of the bullfighters, or matadors, to kill a wild bull, using a sword.

Answer these questions:

1 Name a mountain range in the northwest of Spain.

   _____

2 List three major rivers flowing through the Iberian Peninsula.

   (a) _____ (b) _____ (c) _____

3 What city lies at the mouth of the Douro River? _____

4 Name the ocean that borders Portugal to the west. _____

5 Where is the Strait of Gibraltar? _____

6 What continent is south of Spain? _____

7 Write three facts about the Canary Islands. (Hint: Read page 30 before you answer this question.)

   (a) _____

   (b) _____

   (c) _____

Guess What?

Most of the Canary Islands are made from the remains of extinct volcanoes. Many of the beaches are made of black sand. This comes from the dark volcanic lava that has been worn away by the waves and weather.

The Canary Islands take their name from the Latin word *canes*, which means dogs. The islands were once home to packs of wild dogs. Canary birds also live on these islands.

Exercise B

Fill in the missing words. Use the Word Box to help you.

Spain and Portugal form the Iberian _____. Three seas surround these countries: they are the _____, the _____ and the _____.

The _____ islands lie off the south coast of Spain in the Mediterranean Sea. These islands are called _____, _____ and _____.

The _____ Islands are also owned by Spain, although they lie about 100 _____ off the northwest coast of _____. These islands were formed from the remains of old _____.

The _____ is a major tourist destination in the _____ of Portugal. The capital city of Portugal is _____.

Peninsula	**Mediterranean Sea**	**Ibiza**	**Atlantic Ocean**
Lisbon **south**	**Majorca** **Minorca**	**Bay of Biscay**	**Canary**
volcanoes	**kilometres** **Africa**	**Algarve**	**Balearic**

Exercise C

Make Your Mind Up

Many people argue that bullfighting is a central part of Spanish culture. Others say that it is a cruel form of animal torture. Your local town is deciding whether or not it should allow the bullfighting tradition to continue. The issue will be decided at a town council meeting. Decide whether you support or oppose bullfighting. Write the speech that you will give at the meeting.

_____

_____

_____

_____

_____

_____

_____

_____

_____

_____

_____

_____

_____

_____

_____

Benelux Countries

Colour the Benelux countries.

Use your atlas to help you to fill in the missing labels on the map.

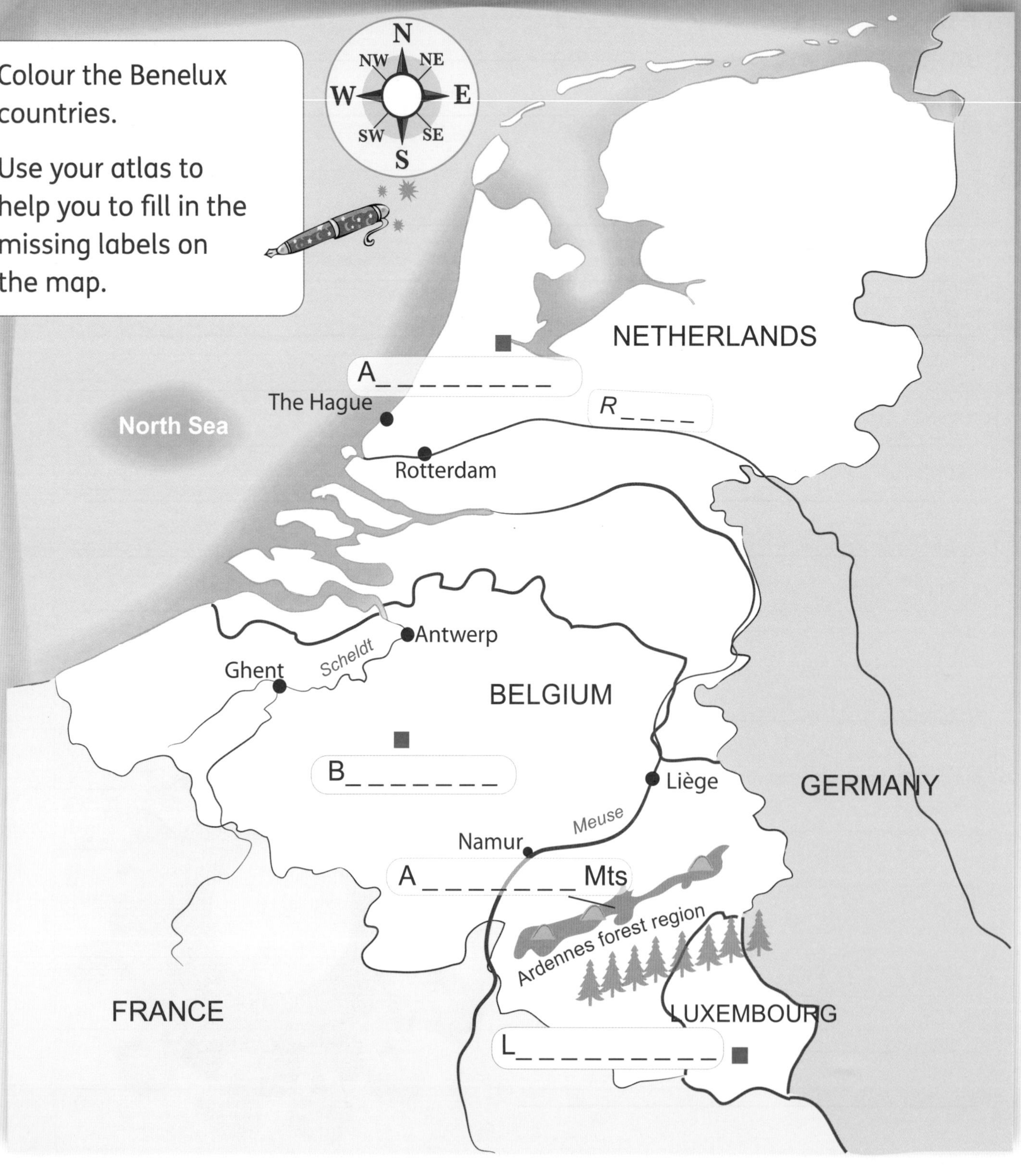

N NW NE
W E
SW SE
S

NETHERLANDS

A_ _ _ _ _ _ _ _ _ _

The Hague

R_ _ _ _ _

North Sea

Rotterdam

Antwerp

Ghent *Scheldt*

BELGIUM

B_ _ _ _ _ _ _ _

Liège

GERMANY

Meuse

Namur

A _ _ _ _ _ _ _ _ _ Mts

Ardennes forest region

FRANCE

LUXEMBOURG

L_ _ _ _ _ _ _ _ _

More about Maps!

The port of Rotterdam is the largest and most modern port in Europe.

The Ardennes is a region of hills and thick forest that extends from eastern Belgium into northern Luxembourg.

The River Meuse rises in northeastern France and flows into southern Belgium. The Belgian section of the Meuse valley, especially around Namur and Liège, is an important industrial and mining region.

The Benelux countries have a temperate maritime climate with cool summers and mild winters.

Answer these questions:

1 Where is the source of the River Rhine? _____

2 Where is the mouth of the River Scheldt? _____

3 How did the Benelux countries get their name? _____

_____

4 Give another name for the Netherlands. _____

5 Where is the capital of the European Union? _____

6 Name the dense forested region to the south of Belgium._____

7 Choose a Benelux country. Write four facts about it.

(a) _____

(b) _____

(c) _____

(d) _____

33

Benelux Countries

Exercise B

Complete this crossword:

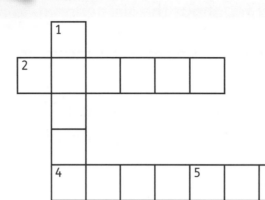

Across

2 This is land that has been reclaimed from the sea.

4 Another name for the Netherlands.

6 This river flows through the city of Namur. Its mouth is in the North Sea.

9 The largest port in Europe is found here.

Down

1 The sea bordering the Netherlands and Belgium.

3 This river flows through Ghent and Antwerp.

5 The capital of the Netherlands.

7 A thick forested region that borders Belgium, Germany and Luxembourg.

8 This is another name for Belgium, the Netherlands and Luxembourg.

Guess What?

Quite a lot of the Netherlands used to be either sea or lake bed. Nowadays, more than half the population lives on land that has been reclaimed from the sea. This low land is known as *polder* land. Big walls, or dykes, have been constructed around the land. Excess water is also drained by an extensive system of canals.

Write the blue words under the correct photograph. Discuss each picture.

1 **Dykes** are still used throughout the Netherlands to reclaim land from the sea.

2 **Canals** have also been used to assist with the drainage of wet land in the Netherlands.

3 **Windmills** are used throughout the Netherlands. They generate energy which is used to pump water.

4 Banking and **financial services** are important industries in Luxembourg.

5 Many people in Amsterdam live on **houseboats**. These are flat-bottomed, barge-like boats.

6 The centre of Brussels is known as the **Grand Place**. This is a large square which dates from medieval times.

Exercise C

Property Project

You own a large building in Rotterdam. You would like to rent this building out as a factory. Design an advertisement to email to local estate agents. Describe why you think your site would be a suitable location for a new company.

Eastern Europe and the Baltic Countries

Arctic Ocean

Ural Mts

RUSSIA

St Petersburg

Tallinn ■
ESTONIA

Valdai Hills

Volga

Riga ■ LATVIA

Moscow ■

LITHUANIA

Vilnius ■

Gdansk ● RUSSIA

Minsk ■

BELARUS

P

Warsaw

Vistula

Krakow ●

Kiev ■

Prague 1

Carpathian Mts

U

Bratislava 2

Ljubljana

Budapest 3

MOLDOVA

4

Chişinău ■

Zagreb

ROMANIA

Caucasus Mts

5

Bucharest ■

Mount Elbrus ▲

SERBIA

6

Black Sea

Caspian Sea

Sarajevo 7 Belgrade Pristina

BULGARIA

Podgorica 9

Sofia

A

8 Skopje

Tirana

1. CZECH REPUBLIC   6. BOSNIA-HERZEGOVINA
2. SLOVAKIA   7. MONTENEGRO
3. HUNGARY   8. MACEDONIA
4. SLOVENIA   9. KOSOVO
5. CROATIA

Baltic Sea

Use your atlas to help you to fill in the missing names of the countries of Eastern Europe.

Skopje, Macedonia

36

More about Maps!

The River Vistula is Poland's longest river. It rises in the south of Poland and flows through Krakow and Warsaw. It enters the Baltic Sea at Gdansk. It is used for transporting coal and timber.

The River Volga in Russia is the longest river in Europe. It rises in the Valdai Hills which are just northwest of Moscow. The Volga is known in Russia as the 'Mother Volga'.

Mount Elbrus is the highest peak in Europe. It is located in Russia and is part of the Caucasus mountain range. Mount Elbrus is formed from an extinct volcano. It is a very popular destination for tourists and mountaineers.

Guess What?

Hitler's invasion of Poland in 1939 was one of the main events that led to the outbreak of World War II. Poland suffered huge losses during this conflict.

In Poland, name days are widely celebrated. Different days are associated with different names. On your name day, your friends and family would gather at your home and give you presents and flowers, just like at your birthday.

Exercise A

Answer these questions:

1 Name the countries that share a land border with Poland. _____

_____

2 What mountain range forms a natural border with Poland and Slovakia?

_____

3 What is the capital city of Croatia? _____

4 What sea borders Poland to the north? _____

5 What is the highest mountain peak in Europe?

_____

6 Describe the course of the River Vistula.

_____

_____

Exercise B

Complete this crossword:

Across

2 Mountain range that forms a natural border between Europe and Asia.

4 Russian people refer to the Volga as '_____ Volga'.

7 Poland's capital city.

8 The largest saltwater lake in the world.

10 Poland's longest river.

Down

1 The sea that borders Poland to the north.

3 These Russian hills are the source of the River Volga.

5 The country that borders Latvia to the north.

6 Major European mountain range stretching from the Black Sea to the Caspian Sea.

9 The capital city of Belarus.

Guess the Location

1 What T is the capital city of Estonia? _____

2 What S is an extremely cold region in Russia? _____

3 What R is the capital city of Latvia? _____

4 What U are the mountains that separate European Russia from Asian Russia? _____

5 What C are the mountains in the south of Poland? _____

6 What V is the longest river in Europe? _____

7 What T was a famous music composer born in Russia? _____

8 What G is a port town in the north of Poland? _____

Tallinn, Estonia

Female Firsts

Marie Curie was the first person in history to win two Nobel Prizes for her work in two different sciences (physics and chemistry). Her achievements are all the more astonishing when you consider that women were not allowed to attend university in her native Poland and that Marie had to travel abroad to study. Research the major events in Marie's life and display them on a timeline.

Marie died in 1934. Design the front page of a newspaper that might have appeared the morning after her death. Remember to include a short biography and to describe her major achievements.

Scandinavia and the Nordic Countries

N
NW NE
W E
SW SE
S

A_____ O_____

Norwegian Sea

Arctic Circle

ICELAND

R_____

Narvik • ▲ Kiruna
Mt Kebnekaise

Lapland

Arctic Circle

Torne

RUSSIA

FINLAND

A_____
O_____

NORWAY
Galdhøpiggen ▲

SWEDEN

Gulf of Bothnia

H_____

O_____

S_____

Lake Vänern

Gothenburg •

Lake Vättern

N_____ S__

B_____
S__

Zealand

DENMARK

C_____

Jutland

GERMANY

Use your atlas to help you to fill in the missing labels on the map.

More about Maps!

Jutland is the name of the peninsula that juts out from northern Europe towards the other countries of Scandinavia. It includes mainland Denmark and parts of northern Germany. The peninsula is divided into two sections by a glacial ridge. Western Jutland is windswept, sandy and has poor-quality soil. Eastern Jutland is much more fertile and has a successful agricultural industry. This region is also more densely populated than Western Jutland.

Lapland is a vast region in northern Europe that lies mainly within the Arctic Circle. It includes parts of Sweden, Norway, Finland and Russia. The arctic climate means that snow and freezing temperatures are common.

Guess What?

Sweden is rich in natural resources. Large forests mean that the timber industry is an important part of the economy. Iron ore is also mined throughout northern Sweden.

The Sami people have lived in Lapland for centuries, surviving the long, harsh winters by herding reindeer for meat, milk and skins. They have their own language and customs.

Exercise A

Answer these questions:

1 Name the gulf that separates Sweden and Finland. _____

_____

2 Which country lies to the east of Finland? _____

3 In which country is Lapland? _____

4 What is life like for people who live in Lapland? _____

_____

_____

5 What is the capital city of Iceland? _____

6 Name a major mountain in Sweden. _____

7 How is Eastern Jutland different from Western Jutland?

_____

_____

Exercise B

Fill in the missing words. Use the Word Box to help you.

Scandinavia is an area in _____ Europe. It is made up of Norway, Sweden and Denmark. These countries, together with Finland and Iceland, are also known as the Nordic countries. _____ is the most southern of the Scandinavian countries. This country is made up of many islands. It shares a land border with _____.

Sweden has a long coastline. There are many lakes in this country. The most well-known are Lakes _____ and _____. There are large areas of forest in Sweden. Mining is a major _____ in Sweden. There is a very large iron ore mine in _____ in the _____ of the country.

A large part of Finland is located within the _____ Circle. The climate is extremely cold with lots of snow. Finland has so many lakes that it is often called the 'Land of a _____ Lakes'.

_____ has one of the longest coastlines in Europe. There are many fjords along the western coast. A _____ is a long narrow inlet usually surrounded by cliffs. It is formed by glaciers.

north	**industry**	**Vänern**	**Arctic**	**fjord**
Norway	**northern**	**Vättern**	**Kiruna**	
Thousand	**Denmark**	**Germany**		

Write the correct caption under each photograph. Use the Word Box to help you. Discuss each picture.

> **Sami people**   **Norwegian fjord**   **mining in Kiruna**
>
> **Lake Vättern**   **Copenhagen**   **reindeer**

Exercise C

Research Time

Choose a city in Scandinavia to research. Present your information using these headings:

- Location
- Tourist attractions
- Weather
- Language

- Currency
- Food
- Interesting facts
- Wildlife

The Balkan States

MOLDOVA

SLOVENIA

Z_ _ _ _ _ _ _

C_ _ _ _ _ _ _ _

L_ _ _ _ _ _ _ _

ROMANIA

CROATIA

BOSNIA-
HERZEGOVINA

B_ _ _ _ _ _ _ _

B_ _ _ _ _ _ _ _

Danube

S_ _ _ _ _ _ _ _

SERBIA

Adriatic
Sea

BULGARIA

Black Sea

MONTENEGRO

P_ _ _ _ _ _ _ _

S_ _ _ _

KOSOVO

P_ _ _ _ _ _ _ _

S_ _ _ _ _

ITALY

T_ _ _ _ _ _

MACEDONIA

A_ _ _ _ _ _

ALBANIA

Corfu

GREECE

Aegean Sea

TURKEY

A_ _ _ _ _ _

Sicily

Rhodes

N
NW NE
W E
SW SE
S

Mediterranean Sea

Crete

View of Greece's capital city

Use your atlas to help you to fill in the missing labels on the capital cities on the map.

More about Maps!

The Balkan Peninsula is in southeastern Europe. It is surrounded by water on three sides.

The peninsula is very mountainous; the major ranges include the Dinaric Alps, the Balkan Mountains and the Pindus Mountains. Many of the mountains are covered in dense forests. The name Montenegro means Black Forest.

Slovenia is one of the richest Balkan states. Its exports include machinery, transport equipment, chemicals and food.

Answer these questions:

1 What is the capital of Serbia? _____

2 Name the sea that borders Bulgaria to the east. _____

3 List three inland countries that are part of the Balkan states.

   (a) _____

   (b) _____

   (c) _____

4 Name the maritime countries in the Balkan states. _____

_____

5 Which Balkan state has the smallest land area? _____

6 How did Montenegro get its name? _____

_____

7 List the Balkan states that are drained by the River Danube.

_____

_____

8 Write three facts about Croatia.

(a) _____

(b) _____

(c) _____

Exercise B

Complete this crossword:

Across

1 One of the richest countries in the Balkan states. It shares a land border with Italy, Austria, Hungary and Croatia.

5 The River _ _ _ _ _ _ flows through ten European countries, to its mouth in the Black Sea.

6 A crescent-shaped country in central Europe. Its capital city is Zagreb.

Down

1 The capital city of Macedonia.

2 A country bordered by Greece, Macedonia, Kosovo and Montenegro.

3 Known as the 'birthplace of democracy'. Its capital city is Athens.

4 The major islands of Greece are Crete, Rhodes and _ _ _ _ _.

Guess What?

There have been many brutal wars in the Balkan countries. These wars mean that the Balkan region is still the least developed and poorest part of Europe.

In June 1914, Archduke Franz Ferdinand of Austria was assassinated in Sarajevo. This is one of the key events that led to the outbreak of World War I.

Exercise C

A family has just arrived at Ljubljana airport. After a few days of skiing, they plan to drive south along the Balkan Peninsula. Travelling along the Adriatic coast, they want to spend two nights in Podgorica and two nights in Tirana. They will then travel to Greece, to explore the historical sites there. After a few days in Athens, they plan to travel to Ankara, Sofia and Bucharest. They want to spend the final weekend of their holiday at the Danube delta, where they will enjoy the famous nature reserve there. Their flight home departs from Bucharest. Use your ruler and a red pen to mark the family's route through the Balkan states on the map. List the countries that they will travel through.

_____

_____

_____

_____

Ankara

Tirana

Bucharest

Asia

Use your atlas to help you to label the oceans, seas and desert.

Circle the Himalayas and the Caspian Sea.

Mark the highest point in Asia using an **X**.

Lake Baikal

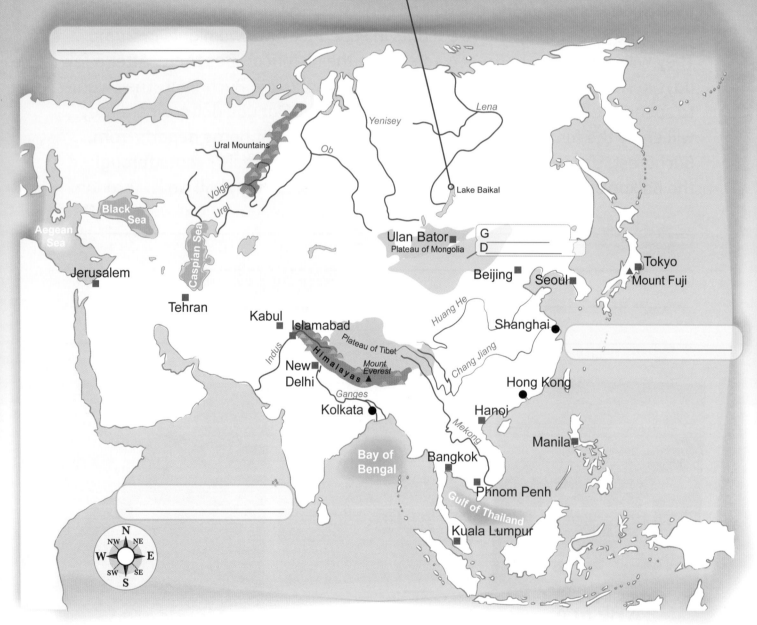

Ural Mountains

Yenisey

Lena

Ob

Volga

Ural

Lake Baikal

Black Sea

Aegean Sea

Caspian Sea

Jerusalem

Ulan Bator
Plateau of Mongolia

G

D

Beijing

Seoul

Tokyo
Mount Fuji

Tehran

Kabul

Islamabad

Plateau of Tibet

Huang He

Shanghai

Indus

Himalayas

Mount Everest

Chang Jiang

New Delhi

Ganges

Hong Kong

Kolkata

Hanoi

Mekong

Manila

Bay of Bengal

Bangkok

Phnom Penh

Gulf of Thailand

Kuala Lumpur

N
NW NE
W E
SW SE
S

48

More about Maps!

Lake Baikal in Siberian Russia is the largest freshwater lake in Asia. It is also the deepest lake on earth. It contains approximately one-fifth of the world's fresh water.

The Caspian Sea is the largest saltwater lake in the world. It borders two continents – Europe and Asia. Some of the largest oil reserves in the world are found under the Caspian Sea.

The Chang Jiang River is the longest river in Asia. It is also the third longest river in the world.

Tibet is a region in southwestern China. It is almost completely surrounded by mountains, including the Himalayas in the south. The sources of many of Asia's longest rivers are found in Tibet.

Guess What?

There are many urban areas with busy factories in Asia. Mineral exports are also very important to the Asian economy – these include petroleum, tin, coal and oil.

Exercise A

Answer these questions:

1 Name a city at the mouth of the River Ganges. _____

2 Where is the source of the River Mekong?

_____

3 What river begins its course in Lake Baikal? _____

4 What is the longest river in Asia? _____

Where does it enter the sea? _____

5 What is the largest saltwater lake in the world? _____

6 Name a city in China, on the east coast, north of the River Huang He.

_____

7 Name a plateau north of the Gobi Desert. _____

8 Write two facts about Asia's economy.

(a) _____

(b) _____

Exercise B

Write the correct name under each photograph. Use the Word Box to help you. Discuss each picture.

G_ _ _   D_ _ _ _ _

T_ _ _ _ _ _   P_ _ _ _ _ _

C_ _ _ _   J_ _ _ _

L_ _ _   B_ _ _ _ _

S_ _ _ _ _ _

M_ _ _ _   E_ _ _ _ _ _

Mount Everest	**Siberia**	**Lake Baikal**
Chang Jiang	**Tibetan Plateau**	**Gobi Desert**

Exercise C

Travel Time

A group of tourists will visit Asia next summer. They hope to visit parts of Central and Southeast Asia. They would also like to spend time in three island countries. The tour group will fly home from a country in northern Asia.

Research this trip:

- Choose the countries that you think the group should visit and explain why. Using a red pen and ruler, mark their route on the map.

- Identify the specific tourist sites on offer in each area.

- Research the best means of travel from each country.

- Provide information on the currency and language of each country.

Africa

Use your atlas to help you to fill in the missing names of the oceans.

Colour the countries that are drained by the River Nile.

Mark the most southerly tip of Africa using an **X**.

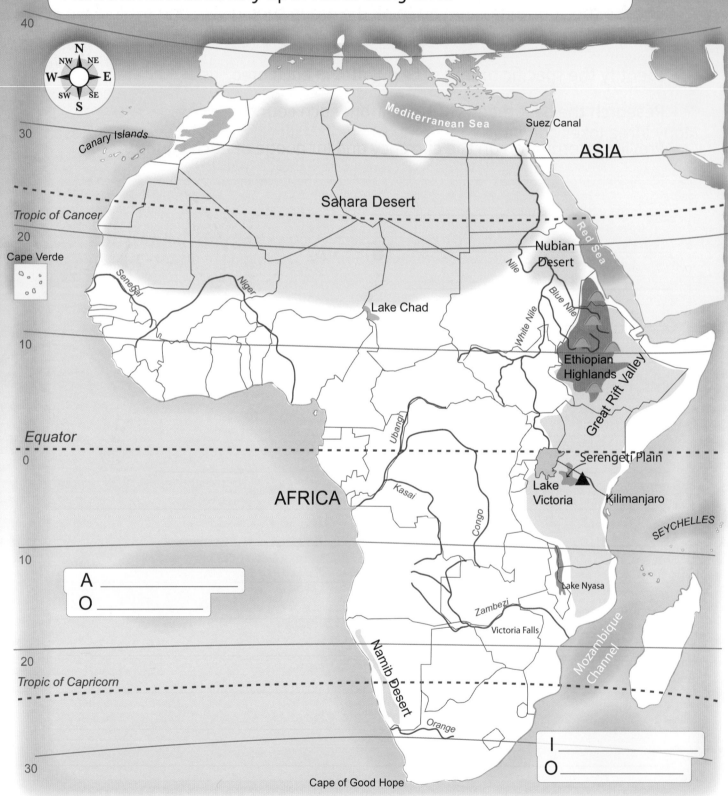

A _____
O _____

I _____
O _____

More about Maps!

Africa has a very varied landscape. The land is higher in the east and south, and lower in the west. The higher land in the east is called the highlands area.

Mount Kilimanjaro, a dormant volcano, is known as the 'Roof of Africa'. It is the highest mountain in Africa. Although it has not erupted recently, steam can still be seen rising from the top.

The Great Rift Valley is a series of great rifts running through southwestern Asia and eastern Africa. Each rift is a deep, long, narrow valley.

Many large lakes can be found in the Great Rift Valley. Lake Victoria, the largest lake in Africa, is found here.

Guess What?

Most of Africa is covered by either grassland (savannas) or desert. The Sahara Desert is the world's largest desert and is almost as big as the continent of Europe! It is one of the hottest, driest places on earth. Rain falls in the Sahara – sometimes quite heavily – but it evaporates quickly. Freezing temperatures at night are quite common from December to February.

Exercise A

Answer these questions:

1 Name three countries drained by the River Niger.

  (a) _____

  (b) _____

  (c) _____

2 Where is the mouth of the River Niger? _____

3 Where is Africa's highest mountain? _____

4 List four countries in Africa that have a coastline.

(a) _____   (b) _____

(c) _____   (d) _____

5 Name a desert in North Africa. _____

Exercise B

Complete this wordsearch:

I	C	O	M	O	Z	A	M	B	I	Q	U	E	G	H
X	H	O	C	G	A	B	O	N	I	L	E	X	C	I
D	R	N	N	P	P	E	A	T	G	I	G	C	H	U
Y	E	S	A	G	H	Q	H	I	B	Q	R	L	A	N
M	J	I	K	P	O	L	R	I	F	T	F	O	D	O
R	S	E	Q	K	I	L	I	M	A	N	J	A	R	O
U	A	H	R	T	V	G	T	N	G	I	I	C	I	B
V	H	K	M	S	S	J	Q	B	W	N	A	T	E	N
S	A	K	H	A	R	T	O	U	M	I	E	K	R	O
U	R	Y	Z	A	M	B	E	Z	I	G	B	Z	R	P
B	A	J	B	M	D	D	B	A	N	E	T	A	I	B
X	E	U	O	Q	O	O	Y	E	T	R	B	Q	K	G
F	G	C	A	I	R	O	R	H	D	I	B	Y	U	R
A	F	A	D	C	Z	E	E	O	G	A	N	D	M	J
N	M	Z	W	R	S	X	L	I	H	O	P	O	O	U

MOZAMBIQUE

CONGO

KHARTOUM

NILE

KILIMANJARO

SAHARA

ZAMBEZI

RIFT

SERENGETI

GABON

CAIRO

NIGERIA

CHAD

Unscramble the names of these African animals. Write the correct name under each photograph. Discuss each picture.

cleanhome

croniesrho

raillog

achethe

acmezenhip

afobflu

Exercise C

Research Time

Working in pairs, investigate an African nation of your choice. You will need to explore the food, tourist attractions, history, natural features, wildlife, major cities, sport, culture, languages and climate of your chosen country. Include some other interesting facts. Draw a large outline map of your country and present your research project to your class.

North America

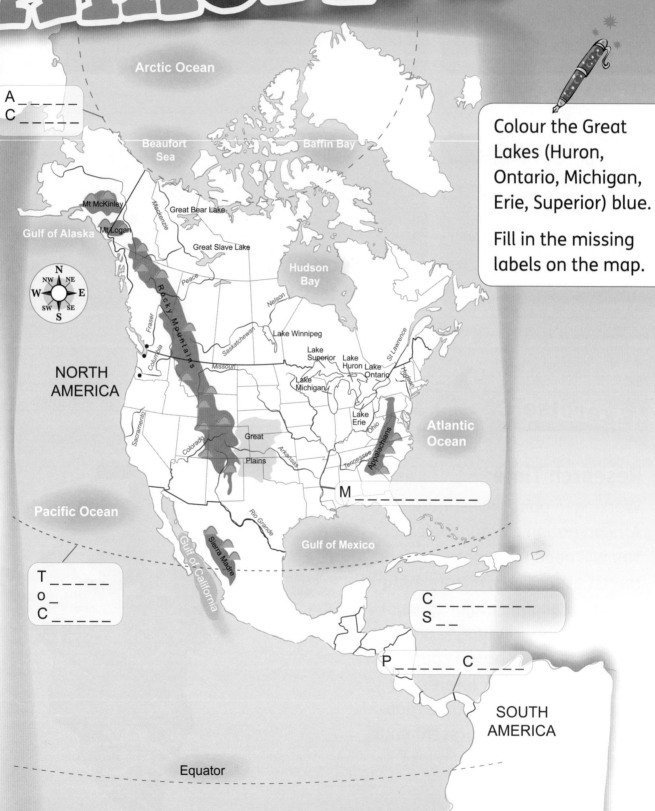

Arctic Ocean

A _ _ _ _ _ _
C _ _ _ _ _ _

Beaufort
Sea

Baffin Bay

Mt McKinley

Great Bear Lake

Gulf of Alaska

Mt Logan

Great Slave Lake

Mackenzie

Peace

Hudson
Bay

Rocky Mountains

Fraser

Nelson

Saskatchewan

Lake Winnipeg

Columbia

Missouri

Lake
Superior

Lake
Huron

Lake
Ontario

St Lawrence

NORTH
AMERICA

Lake
Michigan

Hudson

Sacramento

Lake
Erie

Colorado

Great

Ohio

Atlantic
Ocean

Plains

Arkansas

Appalachians

Tennessee

M _ _ _ _ _ _ _ _ _ _

Pacific Ocean

Rio Grande

Sierra Madre

Gulf of Mexico

Gulf of California

T _ _ _ _ _ _
o _
C _ _ _ _ _

C _ _ _ _ _ _ _ _ _
S _ _

P _ _ _ _ _ C _ _ _ _

SOUTH
AMERICA

Equator

Colour the Great
Lakes (Huron,
Ontario, Michigan,
Erie, Superior) blue.

Fill in the missing
labels on the map.

More about Maps!

The Great Lakes are among the most important inland water masses in the world. They are a group of five freshwater lakes in North America. They form a natural border between the United States and Canada.

Mount McKinley is the highest peak in North America. It is located in Alaska and is part of the Alaska Range. The upper half of the mountain is permanently covered in snow.

The Mississippi-Missouri is the longest river system in North America and the fourth longest in the world.

Guess What?

The Rocky Mountains are a major mountain range in the west of the USA and Canada. The mountains were formed as a result of earthquake and volcanic activity.

Answer these questions:

1 List the five Great Lakes.

(a) _____ (b) _____

(c) _____ (d) _____

(e) _____

2 What is the highest mountain in North America? _____

3 What is the longest river in North America? _____

4 Write three facts about the Rocky Mountains.

(a) _____

(b) _____

(c) _____

5 What lake is east of River Mackenzie? _____

6 Name a large bay in Canada. _____

7 What states does the River Arkansas flow through?

_____

_____

8 How do the Great Lakes benefit the American economy?

_____

_____

Exercise B

Write the correct name under each photograph. Use the Word Box to help you. Discuss each picture.

| Disney World | Empire State Building | Statue of Liberty |
| St Lawrence River | Hollywood Sign | Rocky Mountains |

Match the Name!

Match each state to its nickname by drawing a line between the state and its nickname.

Pennsylvania	Sunshine State
New Jersey	Lone Star State
Massachusetts	Keystone State
New York	Prairie State
Illinois	Empire State
Florida	First State
California	Aloha State
Hawaii	Great Lakes State
Delaware	Evergreen State
Michigan	Golden State
Washington	Garden State
Texas	Bay State

Exercise C

Pen Profile

President John F. Kennedy was the thirty-fifth President of the United States. He was president for just over one thousand days until he was assassinated in Texas in 1963. He was one of the most popular presidents of all time. He had strong connections to Ireland and even visited the country during his time in office. Create a profile of President Kennedy. Research his life, mentioning his childhood, his achievements and his Irish connections. Present your research findings to your class.

South America

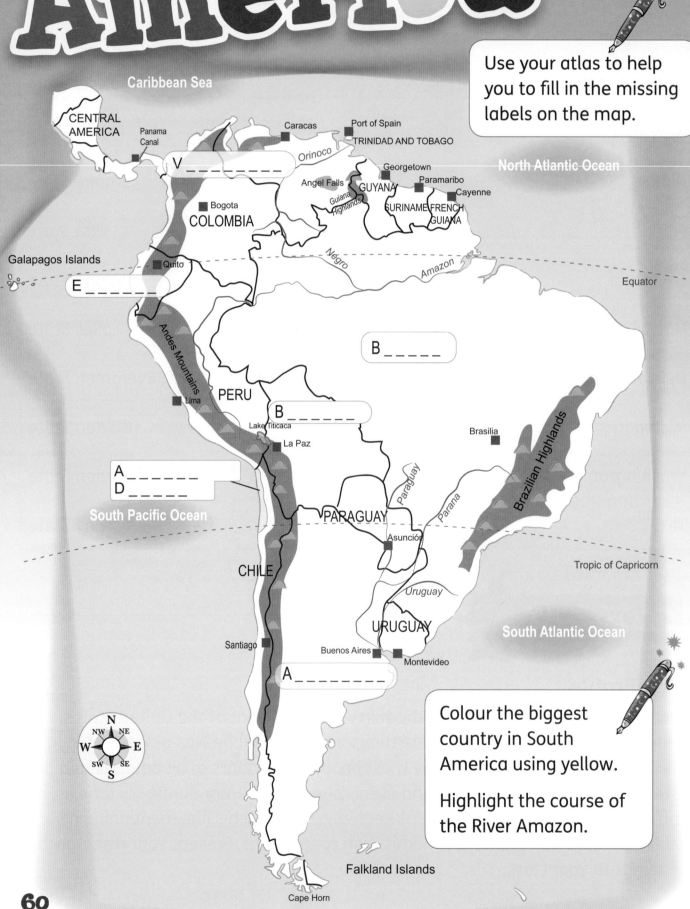

Use your atlas to help you to fill in the missing labels on the map.

Caribbean Sea

CENTRAL AMERICA

Panama Canal

Caracas

Port of Spain

TRINIDAD AND TOBAGO

Orinoco

North Atlantic Ocean

V _ _ _ _ _ _ _

Angel Falls

Georgetown

GUYANA

Paramaribo

Cayenne

Bogota

Guiana Highlands

SURINAME

FRENCH GUIANA

COLOMBIA

Galapagos Islands

Quito

Negro

Amazon

Equator

E _ _ _ _ _ _ _

Andes Mountains

PERU

Lima

B _ _ _ _ _

B _ _ _ _ _ _ _

Lake Titicaca

La Paz

Brasilia

Brazilian Highlands

A _ _ _ _ _ _ _
D _ _ _ _ _

South Pacific Ocean

Paraguay

Parana

PARAGUAY

Asunción

Tropic of Capricorn

CHILE

Uruguay

URUGUAY

South Atlantic Ocean

Santiago

Buenos Aires

Montevideo

A _ _ _ _ _ _ _ _

N
NW NE
W E
SW SE
S

Colour the biggest country in South America using yellow.

Highlight the course of the River Amazon.

Falkland Islands

Cape Horn

More about Maps!

The Andes is the longest chain of mountains on Earth. They run through seven South American countries, along the Pacific coastline.

....

South America also has the second longest river in the world, the Amazon. It carries more water than any other river in the world.

Guess What?

Running down the western coast of Chile is the Atacama Desert, one of the driest places on Earth. In some parts of the desert, rainfall has never been recorded.

....

The most famous waterfall in South America is Angel Falls in Venezuela. This is the highest uninterrupted waterfall in the world.

....

The Amazon rainforest spreads across northern South America. It is the largest rainforest in the world. It is home to one-third of the entire world's animal species.

Exercise A

Answer these questions:

1 What islands lie to the southeast of Argentina? _____

2 Name the mountain range that lies to the west of South America.

  _____

3 Name the mountain range that lies to the east of South America.

  _____

4 Name two countries that are drained by the River Amazon.

  (a) _____

  (b) _____

5 Where is the source of the River Amazon? _____

6 Where is the mouth of the River Amazon? _____

7 Where is the most southerly point of South America? _____

8 Write two facts about the Atacama Desert.

  (a) _____

  (b) _____

Exercise B

Write questions for these answers:

1 _____ ?

It is a desert in the west of the continent. It is one of the hottest, driest places on Earth.

2 _____ ?

It is the world's highest waterfall. It is found in Venezuela.

3 _____ ?

It is a large lake, high up in the Andes.

4 _____ ?

This is the world's longest mountain range. It runs down the west coast of South America.

5 _____ ?

It is the second longest river in the world.

6 _____ ?

They are a group of islands in the South Atlantic Ocean. They lie to the southeast of Argentina.

7 _____ ?

This is the cape at the southern tip of South America.

8 _____ ?

They are islands in the South Pacific Ocean. They lie off the west coast of South America.

King Penguins on the Falkland Islands

Write the correct name under each photograph. Discuss each picture.

| Angel Falls | Lake Titicaca | River Amazon |
| Andes | Atacama Desert | Machu Picchu |

Exercise C

Research Time

The Galapagos Islands are a cluster of small, rocky islands that lie in the Pacific Ocean, about 1,000km off the coast of Ecuador. The islands are home to all kinds of unusual animals such as giant tortoises. These enormous creatures weigh up to 250kg, and can live to be 100 years or older! Many tropical birds live on the islands too, including Galapagos penguins and frigate birds.

Research one animal or bird that lives on the Galapagos Islands. Describe its appearance and its habitat. Find out what it eats and include any other interesting information. Illustrate your work.

Australia and New Zealand

Use your atlas and the Word Box to help you to fill in the missing labels on the map.

Tasmania   Sydney
Great Artesian Basin
Alice Springs   Wellington
Great Barrier Reef

Ayers Rock (also known as Uluru)

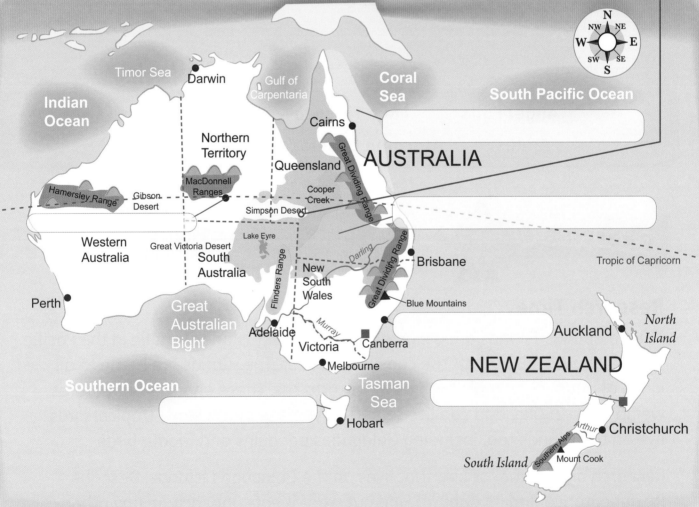

Timor Sea

Darwin

Gulf of Carpentaria

Coral Sea

South Pacific Ocean

Indian Ocean

Cairns

Northern Territory

AUSTRALIA

Queensland

Hamersley Range

Gibson Desert

MacDonnell Ranges

Simpson Desert

Cooper Creek

Great Dividing Range

Western Australia

Great Victoria Desert

Lake Eyre

South Australia

Darling

Brisbane

Tropic of Capricorn

Perth

Great Australian Bight

Flinders Range

New South Wales

Great Dividing Range

Blue Mountains

Auckland

North Island

Adelaide

Murray

Canberra

NEW ZEALAND

Victoria

Melbourne

Southern Ocean

Tasman Sea

Arthur

Christchurch

Hobart

Southern Alps

Mount Cook

South Island

More about Maps!

The Great Dividing Range is a stretch of mountains that runs along the eastern and southeastern edge of Australia. It sends water down to Australia's most important rivers and to the Great Artesian Basin. The Great Artesian Basin provides most of the fresh water for inland Australia.

Lake Eyre is a shallow saltwater lake in central South Australia. It is the largest lake in Australia and it is also the continent's lowest point.

Guess What?

Aboriginal people are thought to have arrived in Australia about 50,000 years ago.

Exercise A

Answer these questions:

1 What is the capital of Australia? Where is it located?

_____

2 Name two oceans that border Australia.

(a) _____

(b) _____

3 Name three states or territories that are drained by the Murray-Darling river system.

(a) _____ (b) _____ (c) _____

4 What is the sea directly northeast of Australia? _____

5 Which tropic line passes through Australia? _____

6 Which hemisphere is Australia in? _____

7 Where is the lowest point in Australia? _____

8 Write two facts about Australia.

(a) _____

(b) _____

Guess What?

Ayers Rock, one of Australia's most amazing sights, can be found in the middle of the Simpson Desert. This is an enormous sandstone rock. It is a sacred Aboriginal site. The Aboriginal term for the rock is *Uluru*.

Australia is an important exporter of agricultural goods like wool, wheat, beef, fruit and wine. The country is also rich in minerals and metals, and is the world's fourth largest producer of gold.

The Blue Mountains, at the southeastern end of Australia, get their name from the blue haze caused by oil droplets given off by the eucalyptus trees. They are part of the Great Dividing Range.

Exercise B

Write questions for these answers:

1 _____?

   It is the longest river in Australia. It flows through eastern Australia to its mouth in the Indian Ocean.

2 _____?

   Major cities on this coast include Cairns, Brisbane and Sydney.

3 _____?

   It is the largest lake in Australia.

4 _____?

   It has two main islands, North Island and South Island, and several smaller ones.

5 _____?

   This is a huge sandstone rock in central Australia. At sunset, the rock appears to change colour from red to purple.

6 _____?

   It is the biggest city in Australia. The Opera House is a popular tourist attraction in this city.

Look at the map. Put these geographical features in order.

1 Number these cities and towns in order from east to west.

Alice Springs ☐   Perth ☐   Brisbane ☐

2 Number these divisions and territories in order from west to east.

Queensland ☐   South Australia ☐   Western Australia ☐

3 Number these cities and towns in order from south to north.

Alice Springs ☐   Adelaide ☐   Darwin ☐

4 Number these mountains in order from east to west.

Hamersley Range ☐   Great Dividing Range ☐   Flinders Range ☐

Exercise C

Aboriginal Dreamtime art is famous. It illustrates the Aboriginal people's story of creation. Each painting shows their traditional beliefs about how their land and people were created. Look at some examples of Aboriginal art. Symbols such as dots and lines appear over and over again.

Paint your own example of Aboriginal art by dipping cotton buds in paint. A sandpaper background can work very well. Use dots instead of lines.

Ireland

Cities and Towns

Use your atlas to help you to fill in the missing names of the cities, county towns and smaller towns.

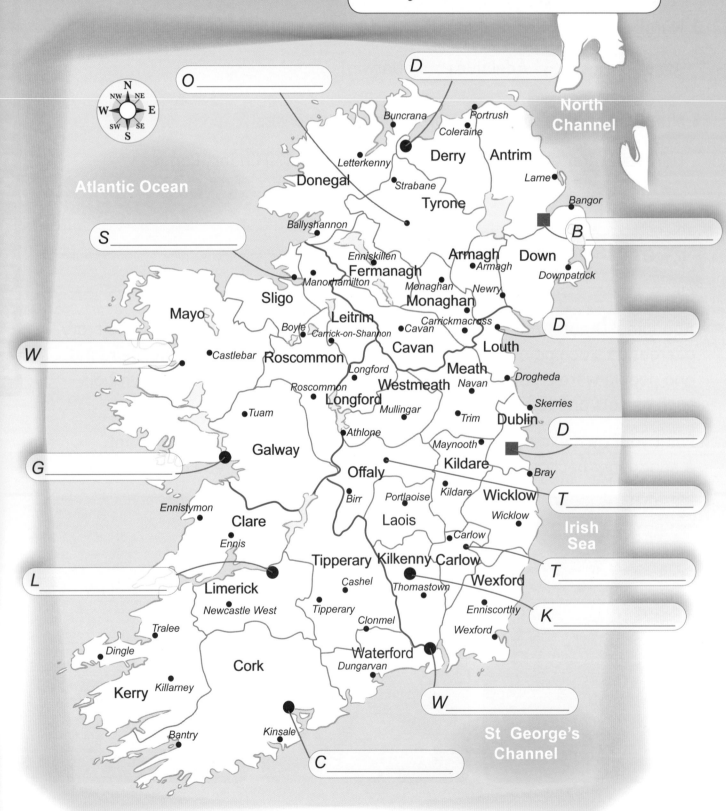

O _____

D _____

North Channel

Buncrana
Portrush
Coleraine
Derry
Antrim
Letterkenny
Larne
Donegal
Strabane
Bangor
Tyrone
Atlantic Ocean

Ballyshannon
B _____

S _____

Enniskillen
Armagh
Down
Fermanagh
Armagh
Downpatrick
Manorhamilton
Monaghan
Newry
Sligo
Monaghan
Mayo
Leitrim
Carrickmacross
D _____
Boyle
Cavan
W _____
Castlebar
Carrick-on-Shannon
Cavan
Louth
Roscommon
Longford
Meath
Drogheda
Roscommon
Westmeath
Navan
Longford
Skerries
Tuam
Mullingar
Trim
Dublin
Athlone
D _____
Galway
Maynooth
G _____
Offaly
Kildare
Ennistymon
Birr
Portlaoise
Kildare
Bray
Clare
Wicklow
T _____
Ennis
Laois
Wicklow
Irish Sea
Carlow
L _____
Tipperary
Kilkenny
Carlow
T _____
Limerick
Cashel
Thomastown
Wexford
Newcastle West
Tipperary
Enniscorthy
K _____
Tralee
Clonmel
Wexford
Dingle
Waterford
Cork
Dungarvan
Kerry
Killarney
W _____
St George's Channel
Bantry
Kinsale
C _____

Exercise A

In what county is each of the following towns?

Town	County
Tuam	
Castleblayney	
Navan	
Cashel	
Castlebar	
Downpatrick	
Letterkenny	
Boyle	
Killarney	

Exercise B

Read the clues and identify the correct town and county.

Clue	Town	County
1 This town's name is a palindrome – it reads the same forwards and backwards.	N _____	_____
2 The Book of Kells is found here.	D _____	_____
3 The *Titanic* was built in the shipyards of this city.	B _____	_____
4 A comedy festival is held here every year.	K _____	_____
5 A town in the centre of Ireland, on the banks of the River Shannon.	A _____	_____

6 A town in Co. Galway, near the border with Co. Clare.	G _____ ____	_____
7 Spanish troops landed here in 1601.	K _____	_____
8 A famous festival is held every summer in this Kerry town.	T _____	_____

These photographs are all associated with places in Ireland. Can you name each tourist attraction? Where would you find it? Discuss each picture.

R _ _ _ _ L _ _

in _____

King J _ _ _ ' _ C _ _ _ _ _

in _____

Á _ _ _ an U _ _ _ _ _ _ _ _ _

in _____

The R _ _ _ of C _ _ _ _ _

in _____

Exercise C

Census Time

A **census** is an official count of the population of a country. Ireland takes an official population census once every five or ten years.

Can you find out when the last census was held in Ireland?

> The populations of our largest cities are approximately:
>
> **Dublin**   525,383   **Waterford**   46,747
>
> **Cork**   118,912   **Galway**   75,414
>
> **Limerick**   56,779   **Belfast**   268,400

Arrange the population of each city in ascending order. Identify the county where each city can be found.

City	County	Population
Waterford	Co. Waterford	46,747

Populations of cities can change over time. Can you think of any factors that might affect the population of an area? List them in the box below. Share your ideas with your group.

Factors that might result in a population increase	Factors that might result in a population decrease

Ireland's Rail Network

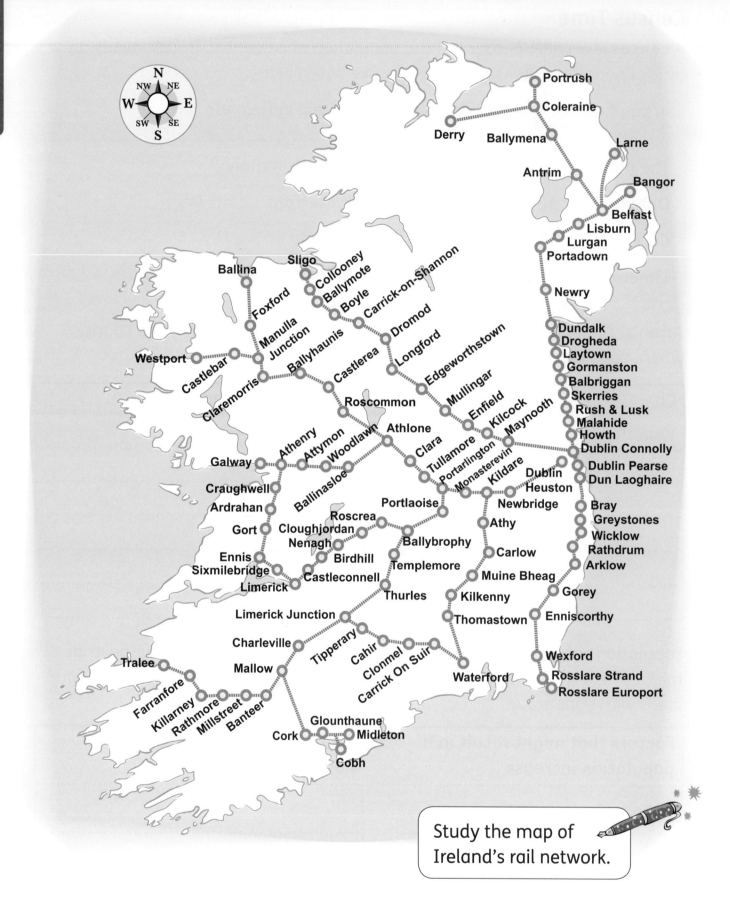

Study the map of
Ireland's rail network.

More about Maps!

Iarnród Éireann is the name of Ireland's railway service operator. It provides a nationwide service that is used by tourists, business people and other travellers.

The InterCity network is shown on the map on page 72. This network links many major cities and towns throughout the country.

Commuter Rail covers commuter routes to Dublin, Cork, Galway and Limerick.

Guess What?

The first railway in Ireland opened in 1834.

The high-speed Enterprise train runs between Dublin Connolly in the Republic of Ireland and Belfast Central in Northern Ireland. It is jointly operated by Iarnród Éireann and Northern Ireland Railways.

The DART (Dublin Area Rapid Transport) train service runs along the coast of the Irish Sea from Malahide or Howth in north County Dublin to as far south as Greystones in County Wicklow. This is an electric rail system. DART trains are recognised easily by their bright green colour.

Exercise A

Answer these questions:

1 What is the name of the railway service operator in Ireland?

_____

2 What is the DART? What does each letter stand for?

_____

3 What is the most northerly town in Ireland serviced by train?

_____

4 List three towns in County Galway that the train network passes through.

(a) _____ (b) _____ (c) _____

5 List three city centre train stations in Ireland's capital city.

(a) _____ (b) _____ (c) _____

6 What is the Enterprise? _____

7 Name the towns serviced by the Athlone to Galway route.

_____

8 Describe the route that you would take if travelling by train from Ballina to Tralee.

_____

Exercise B

These are symbols that are commonly seen at train stations. What does each symbol represent?

_____   _____

_____   _____

_____   _____

In the space provided, design three symbols that could be displayed at a train station. Can your partner guess what each image represents?

Exercise C

All Aboard!

Complete the grid by listing the towns and cities that are covered by each route.

Start	Dublin	Cork	Galway	Belfast
End	Waterford	Roscrea	Portarlington	Dublin

Train Tunes

In your groups, list all the sounds that you could hear in a train station. Can you recreate these sounds by experimenting with your voice, body and instruments? Prepare a one-minute musical soundscape based on a train journey.

Rivers, Lakes, Bays, Islands, Headlands

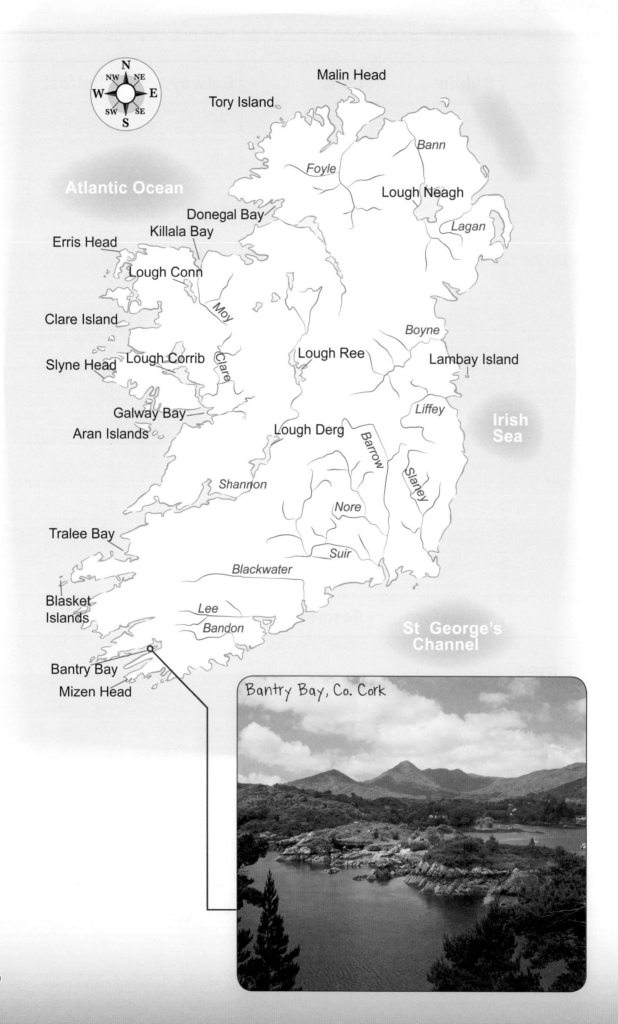

N
NW NE
W E
SW SE
S

Malin Head

Tory Island

Bann

Foyle

Atlantic Ocean

Lough Neagh

Donegal Bay

Killala Bay

Lagan

Erris Head

Lough Conn

Moy

Clare Island

Boyne

Slyne Head

Lough Corrib

Clare

Lough Ree

Lambay Island

Galway Bay

Liffey

Aran Islands

Lough Derg

Barrow

Irish Sea

Slaney

Shannon

Nore

Tralee Bay

Suir

Blackwater

Blasket Islands

Lee

Bandon

St. George's Channel

Bantry Bay

Mizen Head

Bantry Bay, Co. Cork

Exercise A

Write questions for these answers:

1 _____?

The first Viking raid on Ireland took place here in AD795.

2 _____?

This is the collective term for three rivers – the Suir, the Nore and the Barrow.

3 _____?

They are lakes that form when a river starts to meander and a loop becomes cut off.

4 _____?

It is the River Shannon. It measures 242km.

5 _____?

This is a section of land that is connected to the mainland by a narrow strip of land.

6 _____?

They are called Inis Mór, Inis Meáin and Inis Oírr.

Exercise B

Look at the photographs. Unscramble the names of the geographical features. Discuss each picture.

ekla

ramnede

birtaurty

The Course of a River

Use the words in the Word Box to label the diagram.

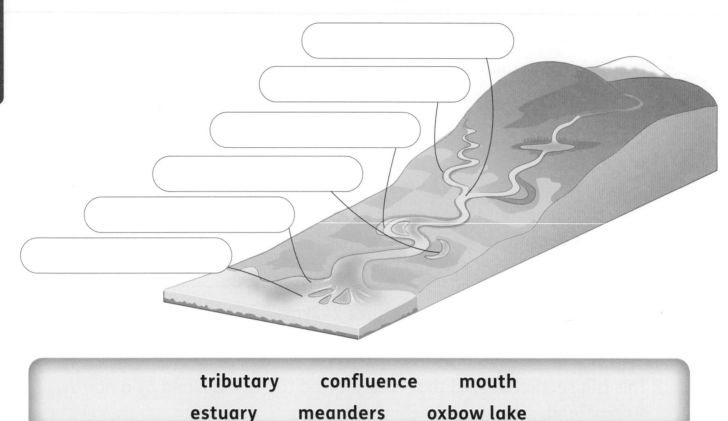

| tributary | confluence | mouth |
| estuary | meanders | oxbow lake |

Complete this paragraph. Use the Word Box below to help you.

The start of a river is known as its _____. It is usually in upland areas such as mountains or hills. As the river flows downhill from the source, it is joined by smaller streams. These are known as _____ of the main river. The point at which two rivers meet is known as the _____. As the river increases in volume, it starts to slow down and swings from side to side. These loops are known as _____. Sometimes, these loops can become cut off from the main river, forming _____. The point where the river enters the sea is known as the _____. When the mouth of the river is on the sea, the fresh water can mix with the sea water. This is known as an _____. Many of our estuaries are bird sanctuaries.

| estuary | mouth | source | tributaries |
| oxbow lakes | meander | confluence |

Mountains

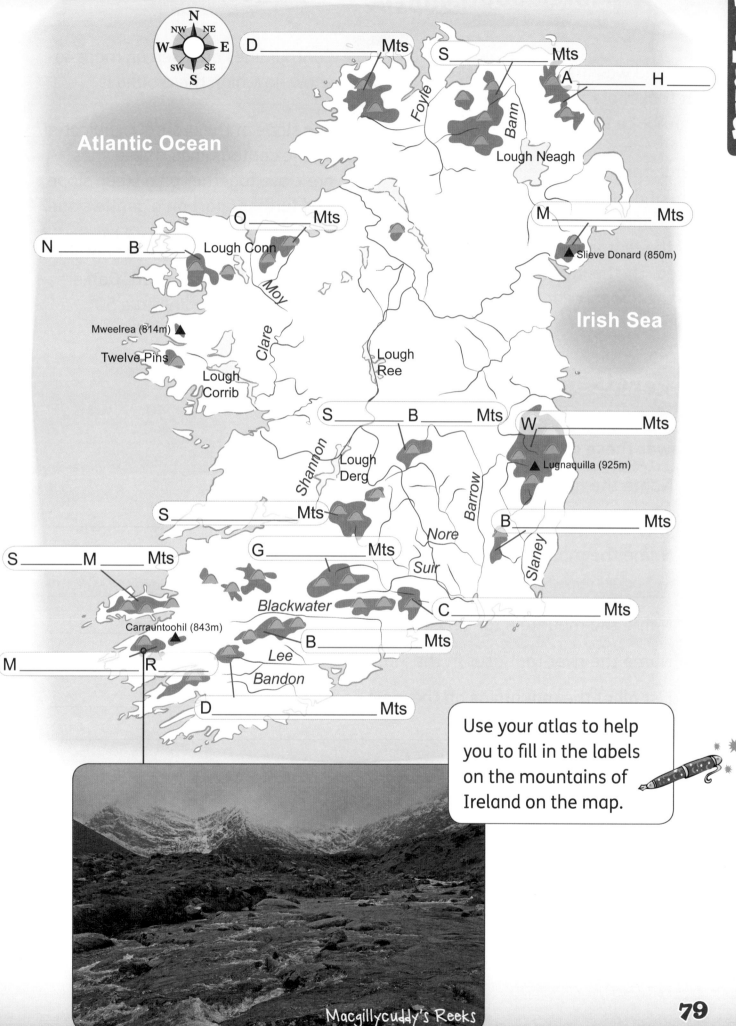

Atlantic Ocean

D _____ Mts

S _____ Mts

A _____ H _____

Foyle

Bann

Lough Neagh

O _____ Mts

N _____ B _____

Lough Conn

M _____ Mts

▲ Slieve Donard (850m)

Moy

Clare

Mweelrea (814m) ▲

Twelve Pins

Lough Corrib

Lough Ree

Irish Sea

S _____ B _____ Mts

W _____ Mts

▲ Lugnaquilla (925m)

Shannon

Lough Derg

Barrow

Nore

Suir

Slaney

S _____ Mts

B _____ Mts

S _____ M _____ Mts

G _____ Mts

Blackwater

C _____ Mts

Carrauntoohil (843m) ▲

B _____ Mts

Lee

M _____ R _____

Bandon

D _____ Mts

Use your atlas to help you to fill in the labels on the mountains of Ireland on the map.

Macgillycuddy's Reeks

79

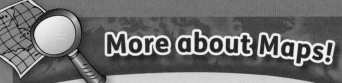

More about Maps!

Ireland was first mapped in 1824. It took more than 2,000 people to complete this job.

Ordnance Survey Ireland (OSI) is Ireland's national mapping agency. An Ordnance Survey map provides details of the features that are in a particular area. The headquarters of the OSI are in the Phoenix Park in Dublin.

Guess What?

Contour lines are used on maps to show how high the ground is.

The slope of the ground is indicated by the contour lines. These lines are close together on a steep slope and further apart on a gentle slope.

On a map, paler-coloured contour lines are 10 metres apart. Darker-coloured contour lines are 50 metres apart.

Exercise A

Answer these questions:

1 Name the mountain range where the River Barrow rises.

_____

2 Name the mountain range where the River Blackwater in Munster rises.

_____

3 Name the mountain range where the River Moy rises. _____

4 Name the river that rises in the Mourne Mountains. _____

5 List all of the mountains on the west coast. _____

_____

_____

6 What is the name of the lines on a map that show how high the ground is?
C _____ l _____.

7 When c _____ l _____ are close together the slope is _____.

8 When c _____ l _____ are far apart the slope is _____ .

Exercise B

Complete the grid.

Province	Highest Peak	County	Height (in metres)
Leinster			
Munster			
Connacht			
Ulster			

Exercise C

More about Mountains

You are a volunteer with Mountain Rescue Ireland. You have been asked to speak to a group of students before they climb a local mountain. Prepare an outline of your speech using the headings below. Write the speech in your copybook.

Equipment _____

_____

Weather _____

_____

Food and drink _____

_____

Clothing _____

_____

Safety _____

_____

Wildlife _____

_____

_____

Britain

N
NW NE
W • E
SW SE
S

Shetland Islands

Atlantic
Ocean

North Sea

Loch Ness
SCOTLAND ● Aberdeen
▲ Ben Nevis

Loch Lomond

■ Edinburgh
● Glasgow

IRELAND

● Newcastle

Pennine Mountain Range

Isle of Man

Irish Sea

● Manchester
● Liverpool

ENGLAND

Severn ● Birmingham

Great Ouse

WALES

● Cardiff
■

Thames ■ London

Calais ●

English Channel

FRANCE

Using your atlas, mark the route from Cardiff to Edinburgh.

Use an **X** to mark the location of the English end of the Channel Tunnel.

More about Maps!

The Channel Tunnel is an underground rail tunnel that connects England to France. It took 15,000 workers almost seven years to complete it. It is the longest undersea tunnel in the world. It runs from Folkestone in England to Calais in France.

The Shetland Islands lie off the northeast coast of Scotland. The islands' latitude means that there is almost continuous daylight during the summer months. The largest island is called Mainland. This is the centre for air and ferry connections.

Guess What?

Stonehenge is an enormous prehistoric monument that is found in Wiltshire in southern England. The monument consists of a circle of standing rocks. Thousands of people gather here each year to celebrate the summer solstice.

Exercise A

Answer these questions:

1 List the three countries that make up Britain.

(a) _____

(b) _____

(c) _____

2 Name the oceans and seas that surround Britain. _____

_____

_____

3 What is the longest river in Britain? _____

In what country is its source? _____

4 Where is the most northerly point in mainland Britain?

_____

5 Name the mountain range north of Ben Nevis.

_____

6 Write three facts about the Shetland Islands.

(a) _____

(b) _____

(c) _____

7 What two countries are separated by the English Channel?

(a) _____

(b) _____

8 Name an island to the west of England. _____

9 In which direction does the Great Ouse River flow? _____

Exercise B

Write questions for these answers:

1 _____?

It is Ben Nevis in Scotland.

2 _____?

It is a country separated from France by the English Channel.

3 _____?

It is a tunnel that runs beneath the English Channel. It links England to mainland France.

4 _____?

It is bordered by four seas – the Irish Sea, the Atlantic Ocean, the North Sea and the English Channel.

5 _____?

In general, the climate can be described as mild with few extremes.

Tube Travels

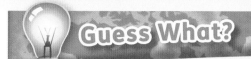
Guess What?

London's underground rail network is known as the 'Tube'. It is the oldest and one of the busiest underground railway systems in the world. It is a quick and easy way to travel around London.

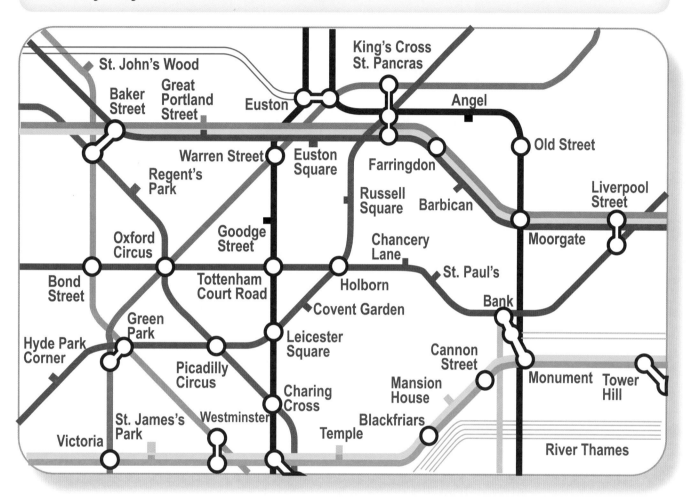

This is a section of the London Underground map. You are staying in a hotel near Liverpool Street. The grid below lists your itinerary for the week. Describe your route from Liverpool Street to each attraction. Remember to describe the direction you are travelling in.

Tourist Attraction	Nearest Tube Station	Route
Buckingham Palace	Green Park	
Madame Tussauds	Baker Street	
Hamleys (toy store)	Oxford Circus	
Big Ben	Westminster	
Abbey Road Studios	St John's Wood	

Guess the Location

Unscramble the words to find the name of each feature below. Discuss each picture.

lhoc nses

neb venis

vierr vesrne

tonesnehge

evirr semaht

fflics fo ovred

Exercise C

Tourist Attractions

There are many famous sights in Britain, such as the Millennium Stadium, Stratford-upon-Avon, the Lake District, Edinburgh Castle, Big Ben, Buckingham Palace, the London Eye, the River Thames, Brighton, Snowdonia, Oxford, Cambridge, Bath, Stonehenge and the Forth Bridge. Research one of these and present your findings to the class.

River Facts

Choose one river in Britain. Using the following headings, describe its course in the box below.

- Source (usually high up in mountains or hills)

- Tributaries

- Cities through which it flows

- Location of its mouth

- Do any estuaries form near the river's mouth?

River: _____

_____

_____

_____

_____

_____

_____

_____

_____

_____

_____

_____

_____

_____

_____

_____

Germany

Use your atlas to help you to fill in the missing labels on the map.

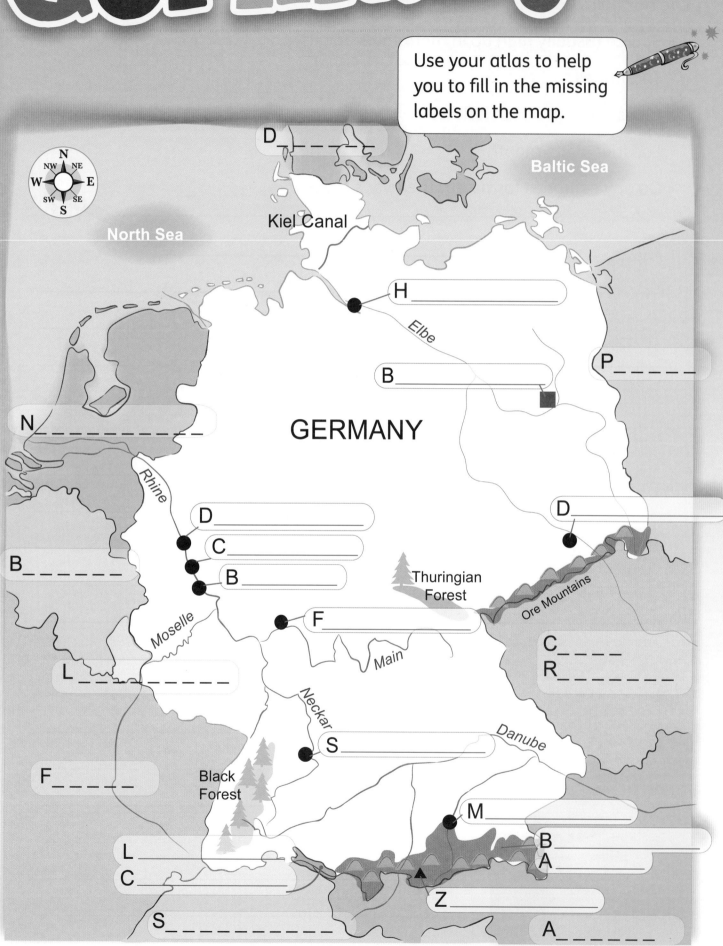

D _ _ _ _ _ _ _

Baltic Sea

Kiel Canal

North Sea

H _ _ _ _ _ _ _ _ _ _ _ _

Elbe

P _ _ _ _ _ _

B _ _ _ _ _ _ _ _ _ _ _ _ _ _

N _ _ _ _ _ _ _ _ _ _ _

GERMANY

Rhine

D _ _ _ _ _ _ _ _ _ _ _ _

D _ _ _ _ _ _ _ _ _ _ _

C _ _ _ _ _ _ _ _ _ _ _ _

B _ _ _ _ _ _ _ _

B _ _ _ _ _ _ _

Thuringian Forest

Ore Mountains

Moselle

F _ _ _ _ _ _ _ _

Main

C _ _ _ _

R _ _ _ _ _ _ _

L _ _ _ _ _ _ _ _ _ _ _

Neckar

Danube

S _ _ _ _ _ _ _ _ _ _ _ _

F _ _ _ _ _ _

Black Forest

M _ _ _ _ _ _ _ _ _ _

B _ _ _ _ _ _ _ _

A

L _ _ _ _ _ _ _ _ _ _ _ _

Z _ _ _ _ _ _ _ _ _ _ _

C _ _ _ _ _ _ _ _ _

S _ _ _ _ _ _ _ _ _ _ _ _

A _ _ _ _ _ _

88

More about Maps!

The Kiel Canal is a 98km-long canal that connects the North Sea to the Baltic Sea. An average of 460km is saved by using the Kiel Canal instead of going around the Jutland Peninsula. This also avoids potentially dangerous storm-prone waters. The canal is one of the most heavily used artificial seaways in the world.

Kiel Canal, Germany

Lake Constance is bordered by three countries – Germany, Austria and Switzerland. More than half of its shoreline lies in Germany. It is a popular destination for water sports.

Guess What?

In September 1939, Nazi forces from Germany invaded Poland. When Hitler refused to withdraw his troops, the Prime Minster of Britain declared war on Germany. Eventually, many other countries became involved and the conflict developed into a world war. The war eventually ended in the summer of 1945.

Following Germany's defeat in World War II, the country was divided into two sections – the Federal Republic of Germany in the west, and the Communist German Democratic Republic in the east. In 1989, a unified Germany was formed with Berlin as the capital city.

German motorways are known as *Autobahns*. They have no general speed limit and are some of the best motorways in the world. The German motorway network is one of the longest in the world.

Sauerkraut and *Bratwurst* is a popular meal in Germany; it is pickled cabbage with sausages.

Exercise A

Answer these questions:

1 Name the maritime countries that share a land border with Germany.

_____

_____

2 Name the inland countries that share a land border with Germany.

_____

_____

3 Name the sea to the northeast of Germany. _____

4 What country is north of Germany? _____

5 Name the major tributaries of the Rhine. _____

_____

_____

6 Identify the source of the River Danube.

_____

7 What mountain range separates Germany from the Czech Republic?

_____

8 Write three facts about the Kiel Canal.

(a) _____

_____

(b) _____

_____

(c) _____

_____

Exercise B

Fill in the missing words. Use the Word Box to help you.

Germany is a country in _____ Europe. _____

is the country that borders Germany to the north. The German flag is a

_____ and it is coloured black, red and yellow. The

_____ is one of the longest rivers in Europe. Its

_____ is in the Black Forest. The _____

lie to the south of Germany, forming part of the border with _____.

The highest peak in Germany, _____, is found here. Germany's

economy is one of the most important economies in the world. Many important

_____ such as Mercedes, Volkswagen and Siemens have their

headquarters here. The _____ in west Germany is a major

industrial heartland. The _____ is one of the most important

rivers in Germany. Tributaries of the Rhine include the Main and the Neckar.

Stuttgart is built on the River

_____.

Frankfurt lies on the River

_____. Some of the

_____ of Germany

include coal, _____

and uranium.

Industry in the Ruhr Valley

Austria	**Zugspitze**	**central**	**tricolour**	**Danube**
source	**natural resources**		**Bavarian Alps**	**Rhine**
companies	**Denmark**	**iron**	**Main**	**Ruhr Valley**	**Neckar**

Write questions for these answers:

1 _____?

Its tributaries include the River Mosel, the River Main and the River Neckar.

2 _____?

It flows from its source in the Black Forest in an easterly direction across Germany.

3 _____?

It flows through Cologne, Düsseldorf and Bonn.

4 _____?

This lake is shared by Germany, Switzerland and Austria.

5 _____?

It is the highest peak in the Bavarian Alps.

6 _____?

It is the most important river in Germany because it transports the country's imports and exports.

7 _____?

It was given this name because the dense conifers do not allow light to penetrate.

8 _____?

It connects the North Sea and the Baltic Sea.

9 _____?

It flows from the Czech Republic, in a northerly direction, through Dresden and Hamburg, to its mouth at the North Sea.

10 _____?

They are called *Autobahns*.

Write the correct caption for each photograph. Use the Word Box to help you. Discuss each photo.

| Brandenburg Gate | Lake Constance | Neuschwanstein Castle |
| Berlin Wall | Zugspitze Mountain | Black Forest |

Exercise C

Extra, Extra – Read All About It!

Choose a famous person who is associated with Germany. Write a short biography for your local newspaper. Answer these questions:

- Why is this person interesting?

- What kind of effect did he or she have on the world?

- List the adjectives that describe this person. What events from his or her life illustrate these qualities?

- What events shaped or changed this person's life? Did he or she overcome obstacles? Take risks?

- Did this person have a positive or negative impact on the world? How and why?

France

Use your atlas to help you to fill in the missing labels.

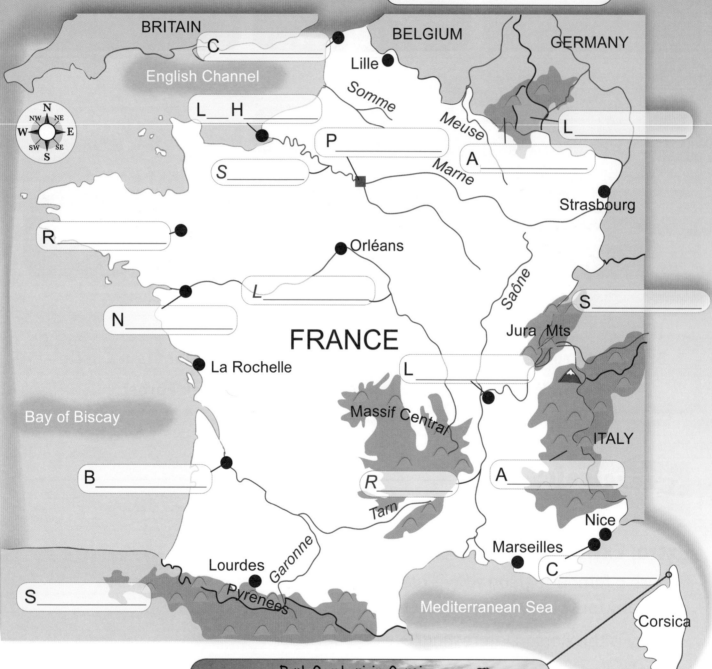

BRITAIN

BELGIUM

GERMANY

C_____

Lille

English Channel

Somme

Meuse

L_____

L__H_____

P_____

A_____

Marne

S_____

Strasbourg

R_____

Orléans

Saône

L_____

S_____

N_____

Jura Mts

FRANCE

La Rochelle

L_____

Massif Central

ITALY

Bay of Biscay

B_____

R_____

A_____

Tarn

Nice

Marseilles

Lourdes

Garonne

C_____

S_____

Pyrenees

Mediterranean Sea

Corsica

Port Centuri in Corsica

94

More about Maps!

The Massif Central region in France contains the largest concentration of extinct volcanoes in the world. There are many hot volcanic springs there which provide the water for mineral water factories. This region covers about one-sixth of France's surface area.

The Pyrenees is a range of mountains in southern France that forms a natural border between France and Spain. It extends from the Mediterranean Sea to the Bay of Biscay on the Atlantic Ocean.

Exercise A

Answer these questions:

Guess What?

A rail system known as *le Métro* runs underneath Paris. The TGV (*Train à Grande Vitesse*) is France's high-speed rail system.

1 Name two countries to the north of France.

(a) _____ (b) _____

2 Name one mountain range on the southern border of the country.

_____

3 What river flows through Paris? _____

4 Name two rivers that flow into the English Channel.

(a) _____ (b) _____

5 Name a city of pilgrimage in the south of France. _____

6 What is the Massif Central? _____

_____

Guess What?

The Louvre in Paris is one of the largest and most visited art museums in the world. Some of the masterpieces exhibited there are by very famous artists such as Monet, Cézanne and Renoir. Leonardo da Vinci's portrait of the *Mona Lisa* can be seen there.

95

Exercise B

True or False?

Tick True or False for each of these sentences. Correct the incorrect facts.

1 The Louvre is a famous museum and art gallery in Paris.

True ( ) False ( ) _____

2 The Rhine is the longest river in France.

True ( ) False ( ) _____

3 The Channel Tunnel is an underground rail tunnel that connects England to France.

True ( ) False ( ) _____

4 Leonardo da Vinci's masterpiece – the *Mona Lisa* – can be viewed in the Louvre Museum.

True ( ) False ( ) _____

5 France's high-speed rail system is known as *le Métro*.

True ( ) False ( ) _____

6 The River Seine flows through Paris and Rouen, to its mouth in Le Havre.

True ( ) False ( ) _____

7 The Bay of Biscay lies along the western coast of France and the northern coast of Spain.

True ( ) False ( ) _____

8 France is a maritime country. Its port cities include Lyons and Strasbourg.

True ( ) False ( ) _____

9 The Massif Central separates France from Spain.

True ( ) False ( ) _____

10 The Vosges are a range of low mountains in eastern France, near its border with Germany.

True ( ) False ( ) _____

Look at the photographs. Write the correct name underneath each picture. Use the Word Box to help you. Discuss each photograph.

| *Mona Lisa* | River Seine | Eiffel Tower |
| Mont Blanc | TGV | Notre Dame |

Exercise C

Vive la France!

Paris is one of the most visited cities in the world. The range of tourist attractions includes the Cathedral at Notre Dame, the Eiffel Tower, the Champs Élysées and the Musée d'Orsay.

Design a brochure advertising two popular tourist attractions in Paris. Provide detailed descriptions of each attraction and information on how tourists can travel to the site. Remember to illustrate your brochure.

Italy

S _____

A _____

Alps

S _____

M_____

Lake Garda

Trieste

F _____

Plain of Lombardy

V_____

Turin

ITALY

P___

Genoa

F_____

Pisa

Arno

Adriatic Sea

Tiber

N
NW NE
W E
SW SE
S

Corsica

A_____ Mts

R_____

N_____

Sardinia

Tyrrhenian Sea

Mediterranean Sea

Palermo

Sicily

M_____

E_____

Use your atlas to help you to fill in the missing labels on the map.

More about Maps!

The Plain of Lombardy is a flat area between the Alps and the Apennines. It is drained by Italy's longest river, the River Po.

The Alps lie to the north of Italy. They are a popular destination for ski holidays, mountaineering and hiking.

Complete the grid. Use the Word Box to help you.

Major cities	
Bordering countries	
Bordering seas	
Major rivers	
Mountain ranges	
Islands	
Active volcanoes	

Sicily	Adriatic	Mediterranean	Slovenia	Milan
Austria	France	Venice	Turin	Pisa	Po
Genoa	Trieste	Switzerland	Florence	Rome
Naples	Palermo	Alps	Mount Vesuvius	Sardinia
Apennines	Tyrrhenian	Mount Etna	Arno	Tiber

Guess What?

The industrial triangle of Italy is located towards the north of the country. The cities of Milan, Genoa and Turin form the three corners of the triangle. This is the wealthiest region in the whole country. The area is located near the major European markets of France, Germany and Britain. Goods can be exported easily and sold to these countries.

Exercise A

Answer these questions:

1 Name two maritime countries that share a land border with Italy.

(a) _____ (b) _____

2 Name two inland countries that share a land border with Italy.

(a) _____ (b) _____

3 Where is the source of the River Po? _____

4 Where is the mouth of the River Tiber? _____

5 Name an active volcano to the south of Italy. _____

6 Name the major European mountain range that stretches from Austria and Slovenia in the east, through Italy, Switzerland, Liechtenstein and Germany, to France in the west. _____

7 Name two islands off the west coast of Italy.

(a) _____ (b) _____

8 Describe the climate of Italy. _____

_____

9 What is the longest river in Italy? _____

Describe its course.

_____

_____

_____

_____

10 Name the mountain range that stretches the length of Italy.

_____

Guess What?

The north of Italy has mild, wet winters and warm summers. There is plenty of flat land available for farming and factories. Soils are rich and fertile and modern machinery is used on the majority of farms.

Exercise B

Write the correct name under each photograph. Use the Word Box to help you. Discuss each picture.

_____

_____

_____

_____

_____

_____

Plain of Lombardy	Mount Etna	Sardinia
Lake Garda	Uffizi Gallery	Pompeii

Exercise C

Down to Business

You are the director of a large international company. You are planning to open a new factory in Italy. Computers will be manufactured there and exported to Europe. Decide where you will locate your company. Write an email to your employees, explaining the reasons for your decision.

Spain and Portugal

B_ _ o_ B_ _ _ _ _ _

B_ _ _ _ _ _

F_ _ _ _ _

P_ _ _ _ _ _ _ _

ANDORRA

Cantabrian Mts

E_ _ _ _

Zaragoza

Douro

Oporto

Sierra de Guadarrama Mts

B_ _ _ _ _ _ _ _

PORTUGAL

SPAIN

M_ _ _ _ _ _

A_ _ _ _ _ _ _

O_ _ _ _ _

T_ _ _ _

Valencia

L_ _ _ _ _ _

B_ _ _ _ _ _ _ _

I_ _ _ _ _ _

Setubal

Sierra Morena Mts

Alicante

Guadiana

Guadalquivir

Murcia

Seville

Sierra Nevada Mts

M_ _ _ _ _ _ _ _ _ _ _ _ _

Almeria

M_ _ _ _ _ _

S_ _

Gibraltar

Canary Islands

AFRICA

Use your atlas to help you to fill in the missing labels on the map.

More about Maps!

Andorra is a tiny, landlocked country. It shares a land border with both France and Spain. Its location high in the Pyrenees Mountains makes it a very popular destination for ski holidays.

The Portuguese town of Setubal is located south of Lisbon. Although its fishing industry has declined in recent years, it is still a major fishing port. In the past, the town was a major supplier of salt to northern Europe.

Guess What?

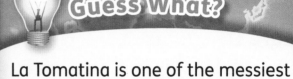

La Tomatina is one of the messiest festivals in the world. It is held in August every year in eastern Spain. Thousands of people travel to this region to throw tomatoes at each other!

Answer these questions:

1 Name two cities on the east coast of Spain.

(a) _____

(b) _____

2 Name the river that flows through Lisbon. _____

3 Name a fishing port south of Lisbon. _____

4 What sea does the River Ebro flow into? _____

5 What Spanish islands lie off the northwest coast of Africa?

_____

6 Name the group of islands off the east coast of Spain.

_____

7 Name the inland country that shares a land border with both France and Spain.

_____

Guess What?

Madrid is the capital city of Spain. It is located in the very heart of Spain. The city is built around the Puerto del Sol, which is the most central square in the city.

Many tourists travel to Madrid to experience some native Spanish cooking. *Paella* is one of Spain's best-known dishes.

The city of Barcelona is one of the main industrial cities of Spain. It is also the biggest port. Many of the buildings are masterpieces. Las Ramblas is Barcelona's most famous street. Local traders and browsing tourists make this a very busy area of the city.

Picture It

Unscramble these words. Write the correct caption under each photograph below.

- aL motTania
- saL maRblsa
- naCraeis
- ordtaaM
- malFneoc
- lPleaa

Complete this crossword:

Across

1 Popular Spanish dish.

4 Capital city of Spain.

5 A piece of land that juts out into the sea and is surrounded by sea on three sides.

8 A country high in the Pyrenees mountains, on the French-Spanish border.

9 Capital city of Portugal.

Down

1 Official language of Portugal.

2 La _____ is known as the messiest festival in the world!

3 This currency is used throughout the Iberian Peninsula.

6 Popular holiday destination in Portugal.

7 Major fishing port on the west coast of Portugal.

8 This continent lies to the south of the Iberian Peninsula.

Lisbon, Portugal

Exercise B

True or False?

Tick the box, True or False. Correct any incorrect facts.

1 The River Tagus flows in a westerly direction towards its mouth in the Atlantic Ocean.

True ◯ False ◯ _____

2 The three Balearic Islands are Ibiza, Majorca and Lanzarote.

True ◯ False ◯ _____

3 The Pyrenees mountain range separates France from Spain.

True ◯ False ◯ _____

4 Flamenco dancing and bullfighting are popular pastimes in Spain.

True ◯ False ◯ _____

5 Spain, Portugal and Greece form the Iberian Peninsula.

True ◯ False ◯ _____

6 The Bay of Biscay lies to the south of Spain.

True ◯ False ◯ _____

7 The source of the River Ebro lies in the Cantabrian Mountains.

True ◯ False ◯ _____

8 Andorra is a maritime country.

True ◯ False ◯ _____

9 Madrid is the capital of Spain.

True ◯ False ◯ _____

10 The narrow stretch of water between Spain and Africa is called the Strait of Gibraltar.

True ◯ False ◯ _____

Exercise C

Design Time

The Spanish artist Antoni Gaudi is responsible for much of the beautiful architecture in Barcelona. He covered many of his buildings in coloured mosaics.

Create a streetscape in the style of Gaudi. Draw a series of buildings close together. Add architectural details such as domed roofs. Colour each building using bright colours. If you like, you can add glitter and plastic gemstones to create a mosaic effect. Add plants and shrubs to the areas in front of your buildings. Sketch a plan of your streetscape below.

Benelux Countries

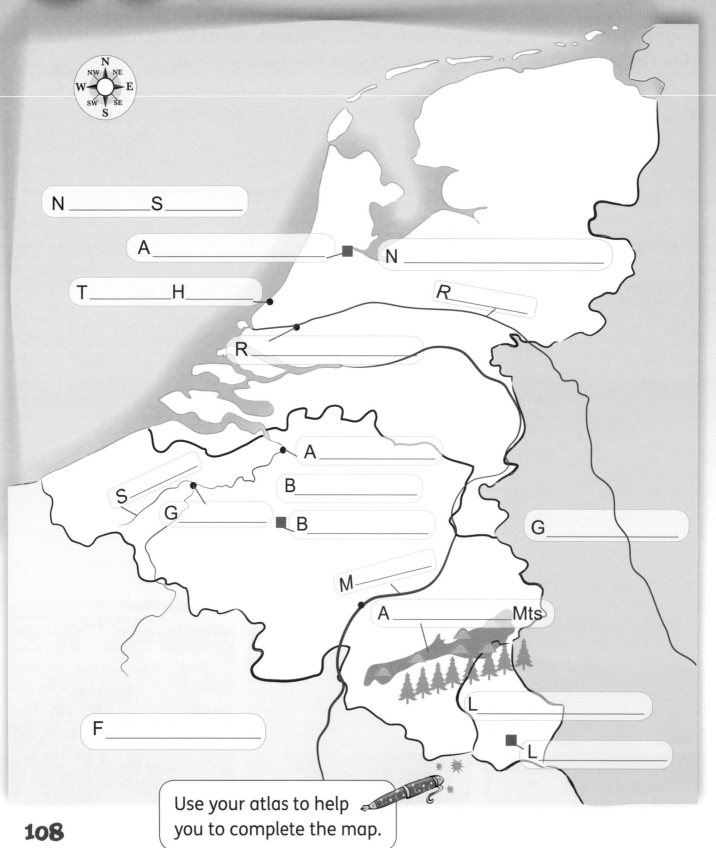

N_____ S_____

A_____

T_____H_____

R_____

N_____

R_____

A_____

S_____

B_____

G_____

G_____

B_____

M_____

A_____Mts

L_____

F_____

L_____

Use your atlas to help you to complete the map.

More about Maps!

The River Rhine is one of the longest and most important rivers in Europe. It rises in the Swiss Alps and flows generally north before emptying into the North Sea at Rotterdam.

The River Meuse is a major European river, rising in France, and flowing through Belgium and the Netherlands, before draining into the North Sea.

Guess What?

The Rhine has more castles along its length than any other river in the world. It also carries more traffic than any other river in the world.

Exercise A

Answer these questions:

1 What river is Antwerp built on?

_____

2 What body of water lies to the west of Belgium?

_____

3 Describe the climate of the Benelux countries. _____

_____

4 Name a maritime country to the north of Luxembourg.

_____

5 Name the forested region that forms part of the land border between Luxembourg, Belgium and Germany. _____

6 Name two rivers that flow in a westerly direction through the Netherlands.

(a) _____   (b) _____

7 Write three facts about the River Rhine.

(a) _____

(b) _____

(c) _____

8 Name two countries that border the Netherlands.

(a) _____ (b) _____

9 What is the capital of Luxembourg? _____

10 Where is the largest port in Europe? _____

Why is this a suitable location for a major port city? _____

_____

Exercise B

Guess What?

The Hague is the third largest city in the Netherlands, after Amsterdam and Rotterdam. More than 150 international organisations have their headquarters there, including the International Court of Justice and the International Criminal Court.

Guess the Location

1 This is a very bicycle-friendly city. There are many tourist attractions here such as Anne Frank's house and the many canals. You can also see many of Van Gogh's paintings in the Rijksmuseum.

_____

2 This city lies in the northeast of Belgium. It is known as the diamond capital of the world.

_____

3 This is the second longest river in Europe. It rises in the Swiss Alps and flows for 1,233km to its mouth in the North Sea. _____

4 This is the second largest city in the Netherlands. It lies on the River Rhine. It is the largest port in Europe. _____

5 This is the third largest city in the Netherlands. Many organisations working in the fields of peace and justice have their headquarters here.

_____

6 This is a small landlocked country. It is bordered by Germany, France and Belgium. It is a very important country for banking and finance. The capital city has the same name as the country. _____

7 Several languages are spoken in this city. The headquarters of the European Union can be found here. _____

8 Much of this country lies below sea level. More than half the population lives on *polder* land – land that has been reclaimed from the sea. A system of canals, dykes and water pumps prevents the North Sea from flooding the *polder* land. _____

9 The source of this river is in France. It flows through Belgium and the Netherlands. Its mouth is in the North Sea. The Belgian city of Namur lies on this river. _____

True or False?

Five of these sentences are false. Can you find them? Correct any incorrect facts.

1 The headquarters of the International Court of Justice and the International Criminal Court are located in The Hague.

True ◯ False ◯ _____

2 The Netherlands is a small country located between Belgium and Germany in Western Europe.

True ◯ False ◯ _____

3 Belgium is a very mountainous country with several major mountain ranges.

True ◯ False ◯ _____

4 The mouth of the River Rhine is in the Baltic Sea.

True ◯ False ◯ _____

5 Windmills were built throughout the Netherlands to assist with land drainage.

True ◯ False ◯ _____

6 Bruges is a popular tourist destination in Belgium – it is often known as the Venice of the North.

True ◯ False ◯ _____

7 The River Rhine flows through six countries, including the three Benelux countries.

True ◯   False ◯   _____

8 Luxembourg is a maritime country with several major port cities.

True ◯   False ◯   _____

9 Luxembourg's central location and multilingual population have helped it to become a leading financial centre.

True ◯   False ◯   _____

10 Bicycles are a familiar part of everyday life in the Netherlands.

True ◯   False ◯   _____

Exercise C

Research Time

Divide your class into three groups. Each group will investigate a different Benelux country. Assign a topic to each pupil in the group. You will need to explore the food, tourist attractions, natural features, major cities, sport, culture, languages and climate of your chosen country. Are there any famous people living there? Include some other interesting facts. Draw a large outline map of your country on a separate sheet of paper and present your research project to your class. List your ideas in the web diagram on the next page.

Tulips in the Netherlands

Climate
_____
_____
_____

Languages
_____
_____
_____

Food
_____
_____
_____
_____

Sport
_____
_____
_____

Country
_____

Culture
_____
_____
_____
_____

Major Cities
_____
_____
_____

Tourist Attractions
_____
_____
_____

Famous People
_____
_____
_____

Natural Features
_____
_____
_____

Eastern Europe and the Baltic Countries

Arctic Ocean

N
NW NE
W E
SW SE
S

Siberia

U

M

RUSSIA

Gulf of Finland
Tallinn
ESTONIA

Valdai Hills

Volga

Gulf of Riga
Riga ■ LATVIA

Baltic Sea

LITHUANIA
Vilnius ■

RUSSIA

POLAND
Warsaw

Minsk ■
BELARUS

Moscow ■

Vistula
Krakow
Prague 1
Carpathian Mts
Bratislava 2
3
Ljubljana
Budapest
4 ■ Zagreb
5
SERBIA
6
Belgrade
Saralevo 7 Pristina
Podgorica ■ 10
9 ■ Skopje
Tirana ■ 8

Kiev ■

UKRAINE

MOLDOVA
Chișinău ■

ROMANIA
Bucharest ■

BULGARIA
Sofia ■

Black Sea

Volgograd

C
M

Mount Elbrus

C
S

1. CZECH REPUBLIC
2. SLOVAKIA
3. HUNGARY
4. SLOVENIA
5. CROATIA

6. BOSNIA-HERZEGOVINA
7. MONTENEGRO
8. MACEDONIA
9. ALBANIA
10. KOSOVO

Use your atlas to help you to fill in the missing labels on the map.

Kiev, Ukraine

More about Maps!

The Caspian Sea is the world's largest inland sea. It lies on the border between Europe and Asia. The River Volga is a major tributary of the Caspian Sea.

The Ural Mountains separate Europe from Asia. They are rich in mineral deposits such as coal and precious stones.

Guess What?

Pope John Paul II was born in Krakow in Poland. He died in 2005.

Warsaw dates from the 13th century. Much of the city was destroyed during heavy fighting in World War II. It was restored after the war and is now considered to be one of the most beautiful cities in the world.

Exercise A

Answer these questions:

1 List the countries that share a land border with Belarus. _____

_____

2 What is the currency of Poland? _____

3 What is the currency of Russia? _____

4 What mountain range lies just south of Krakow?_____

5 List two facts about the Caspian Sea.

(a) _____

(b) _____

6 What geographical feature separates Estonia from Finland?

_____

7 List the European countries that share a land border with Russia.

_____

8 What is the highest peak in Europe? _____

Where is it located?_____

Exercise B

Fill in the missing words.

1 The coldest area of Russia is known as _____. Many famous
m_____ composers such as T_____ and
Rachmaninoff were born in Russia.

2 Estonia is bordered by _____ and Russia. The flag is
_____, black and _____.

3 Latvia is one of the _____ Countries. The official language is
_____.

4 The River N_____ flows through the capital city of Lithuania.

5 The River _____ flows through Warsaw and enters the
_____ Sea. Marie Curie, the famous _____,
was born in Warsaw.

6 The C_____ Mountains are found in the southwest of Ukraine.
The Black Sea lies to the s_____ of the country.
U_____ is the official language of Ukraine.

7 Moldova is a completely _____ country. It is bordered by
Romania and _____.

Use the map on page 114 to help you to complete the grid.

Country	Capital
Russia	
Estonia	
Latvia	
Lithuania	
Poland	
Ukraine	
Moldova	

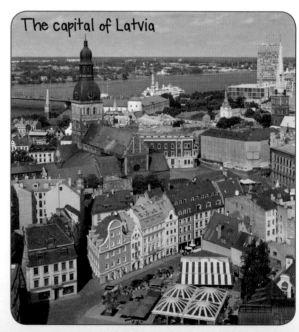

The capital of Latvia

Exercise C

All Aboard

The Trans-Siberian Railway is the longest rail line in the world. One of the rail lines begins in Moscow in the west and finishes in the port city of Vladivostok in the east. Along the way are some of Russia's most famous sights, including Lake Baikal and the plains of Siberia. The journey takes in eighty-seven Russian cities and passes through seven time zones. The fastest train trip along the line takes six days without stopping. Imagine that you are a reporter on this journey. Write a report on some of the sights you have seen. Describe what life is like for passengers.

_____

_____

_____

_____

_____

_____

_____

_____

_____

_____

_____

_____

_____

_____

_____

Scandinavia and the Nordic Countries

Use your atlas to help you to complete the map.

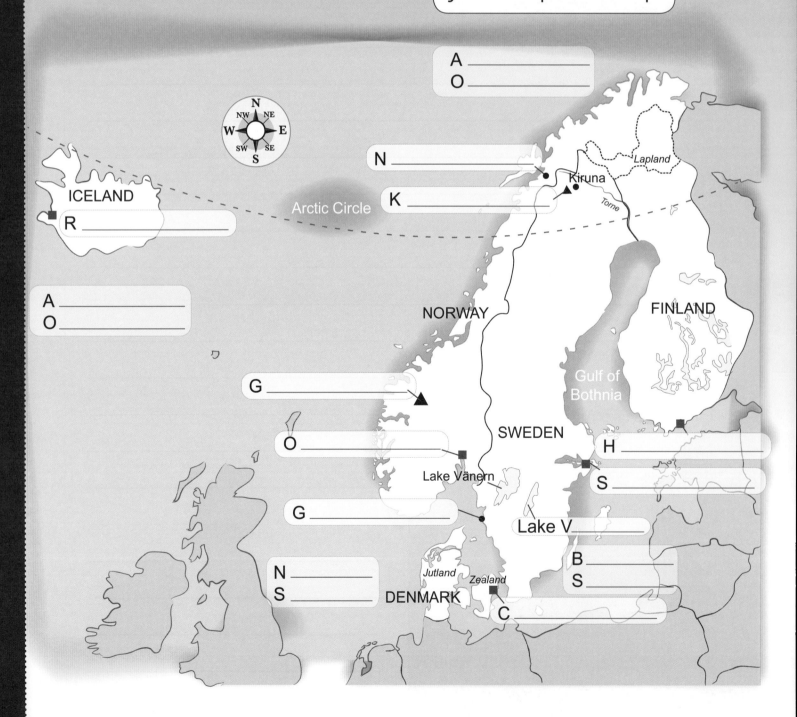

A _____
O _____

N _____

K _____

ICELAND

R _____

Arctic Circle

Kiruna

Lapland

Torne

A _____
O _____

NORWAY

FINLAND

Gulf of Bothnia

G _____

SWEDEN

O _____

H _____

Lake Vänern

S _____

G _____

Lake V_____

N _____
S _____

Jutland   Zealand

DENMARK

B _____
S _____

C _____

More about Maps!

The northern polar region is called the **Arctic**. This is one of the world's coldest places. The Arctic Ocean is an enormous ocean surrounded by land. Most of the ocean is constantly frozen.

The Arctic Circle is an imaginary line showing the boundary of the Arctic region. The Inuit people live north of the Arctic Circle.

Guess What?

Gothenburg is the second largest city in Sweden. It is located on Sweden's west coast and it is the busiest port city in the Nordic countries.

The famous writer Hans Christian Andersen was from Denmark. Children all over the world are familiar with his fairytales. His best-loved stories include *Thumbelina*, *The Ugly Duckling* and *The Little Mermaid*. The Little Mermaid statue in Copenhagen Harbour is one of the most popular tourist attractions in Denmark.

Exercise A

Answer these questions:

1 Name the capital city of Iceland. _____

2 Name the capital city of Finland. _____

3 Write two facts about the Arctic.

  (a) _____

  (b) _____

4 Describe the location of Lapland. _____

_____

5 In which hemisphere is Scandinavia?

_____

6 Name two major lakes in Sweden.

(a) _____ (b) _____

7 Name the sea on the east coast of Sweden. _____

8 Name a major mountain range in Norway. _____

9 What is a fjord? _____

_____

Exercise B

Alphabet Quiz

Work in pairs. Some of the answers can be found in this chapter. Other questions are more difficult and you will need to research the answers. Working with your partner, see how many questions you can answer now. Discuss how you will find the answers to the other questions.

What **A** _____ is the imaginary line that shows the boundaries of the Arctic region?

What **B** _____ is a gulf on the eastern coast of Sweden?

What **C** _____ is the capital city of Denmark?

What **D** _____ is a type of farming that is very common in Denmark?

What **E** _____ is a country south of Finland?

What **F** _____ is a feature found on the west coast of Norway?

What **G** _____ is the second largest city in Sweden?

What **H** _____ is the capital city of Finland?

What **I** _____ is a common feature found in Denmark?

What **J** _____ is a peninsula that juts out from
Northern Europe towards the other parts of Scandinavia?

What **K** _____ is a mountain range in the north of Sweden?

What **L** _____ is the most northerly part of Sweden?

What **M** _____ is an important industry in Scandinavia?

What **N** _____ is a port in the north of Norway?

What **O** _____ is the capital city of Norway?

What **P** _____ , along with islands,
forms the country of Denmark?

What **Q** _____ is a monarch and a head of state in Sweden?

What **R** _____ is the capital city of Iceland?

What **S** _____ depicting the Little Mermaid
is found in the harbour of Copenhagen?

What **T** _____ is one of Sweden's most important resources?

What **U** _____ is a river in Sweden?

What **V** _____ is a major lake in Sweden?

What **W** _____ are the types of product
made from timber in Scandinavia?

What **Y** _____ is the colour of the cross on the Swedish flag?

What **Z** _____ is the island on which Copenhagen is built?

True or False?

Five of these facts are false. Can you find them? Rewrite any incorrect facts.

1 Norway is situated in the western part of the Scandinavian peninsula.

True ⬭　False ⬭ _____

2 The capital and largest city in Sweden is Stockholm.

True ⬭　False ⬭ _____

3 Sweden occupies the eastern part of the Scandinavian peninsula.

True ⬭　False ⬭ _____

4 Sweden is the most northerly European country.

True ⬭　False ⬭ _____

5 Iceland lies in the north Atlantic Ocean, west of Greenland. It does not touch the Arctic Circle.

True ⬭　False ⬭ _____

6 Iceland is not known for its volcanic activity.

True ⬭　False ⬭ _____

7 The capital of Finland is Espoo.

True ⬭　False ⬭ _____

8 The Scandinavian peninsula is bordered by the Gulf of Bothnia, the Baltic Sea, the North Sea, the Atlantic Ocean and the Arctic Ocean.

True ⬭　False ⬭ _____

9 The Arctic Circle is an imaginary circle on the surface of the earth. It marks the most northerly point at which the sun can be seen during the summer solstice.

True ⬭　False ⬭ _____

10 The *aurora borealis* or northern lights are a luminous display of different coloured lights.

True ⬭　False ⬭ _____

Write the correct title under each photo. Use the Word Box to help you. Discuss each picture.

| Inuit | Norwegian fjord | Little Mermaid |
| Atlantic puffins | tundra | *aurora borealis* |

Exercise C

Research Time

Hans Christian Andersen was a famous Danish author. Research the life of Hans Christian Anderson and present your findings to the class. Use these headings to help you:

- Early life
- His achievements
- His legacy

Choose one of Hans Christian Andersen's fairytales and rewrite the story in your own words. Illustrate each page. Read your story to children in younger classes.

The Balkan States

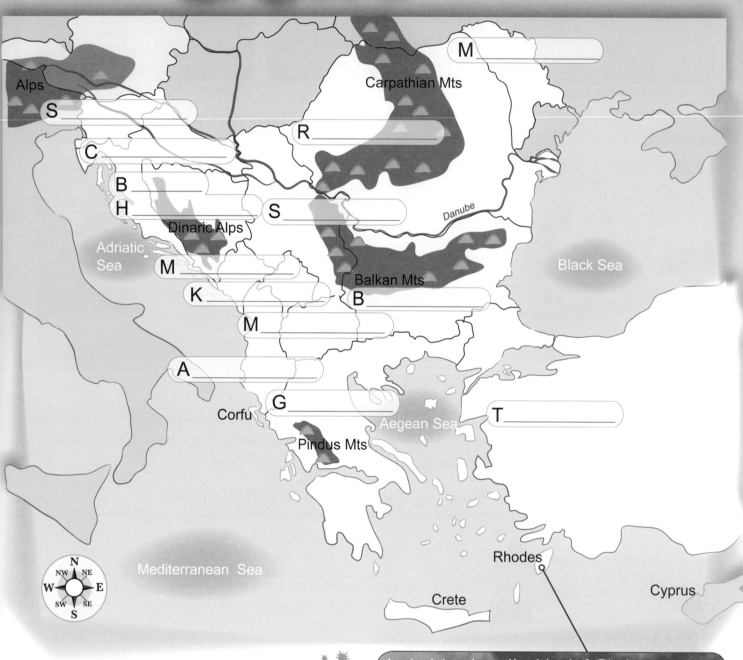

Alps

M _____

Carpathian Mts

S _____

R _____

C _____

B _____

H _____

S _____

Dinaric Alps

Danube

Adriatic Sea

Black Sea

M _____

K _____

Balkan Mts

B _____

M _____

A _____

Corfu

G _____

Aegean Sea

T _____

Pindus Mts

N
NW NE
W   E
SW SE
S

Mediterranean Sea

Rhodes

Crete

Cyprus

Use your atlas to help you to complete the map.

Colour Greece red.

Colour Moldova blue.

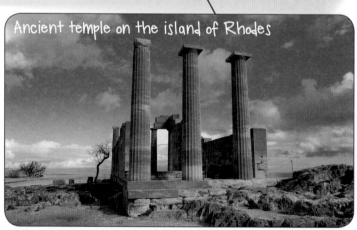

Ancient temple on the island of Rhodes

More about Maps!

Mountains ranging up to 3,000m high make up most of the land area of the Balkan states.

The area along the coasts and along the valleys of the River Danube consists largely of lowlands and plains. The River Danube separates the Carpathian Mountains, the Balkan Mountains and the Alps.

The Dinaric Alps extend along the coast of the Adriatic Sea. Cold winds from this mountain range mean that winters in Bosnia-Herzegovina can be bitterly cold.

Guess What?

The word 'Balkan' comes from a Turkish word that means 'wooded mountain'.

The Pindus range is Greece's main mountain range. It runs from the Albanian border to northwest Greece. It is often known as the 'spine of Greece'.

Exercise A

Answer these questions:

1 How did the Balkan states get their name?

   _____

2 Name the mountain range that forms the 'spine of Greece'.

   _____

3 List the Balkan states that have no coastline. _____

   _____

4 List the Balkan states that are maritime states. _____

   _____

5 Write the names of the countries that share a land border with the Balkan states. _____

   _____

125

6 Name the major river that flows in an easterly direction through the Balkans.

_____

7 Name a major mountain range to the east of the Balkan states.

_____

8 Where is the mouth of the River Danube? _____

Exercise B

Guess the Location

1 This is the second longest river in Europe. Its source is in Germany's Black Forest and it flows for approximately 2,850km to its mouth in the Black Sea. It passes along or through Germany, Austria, Slovakia, Hungary, Croatia, Serbia, Bulgaria, Romania, Ukraine and Moldova.

_____

2 This capital city lies in the west of Albania. It was once a heavily polluted city but in recent years, residents have worked to make it a more attractive place to live.

_____

3 Mother Teresa was born in this capital city in 1910.

_____

4 This country spreads over two continents. The smaller, northwestern region is considered to be part of the Balkan states.

_____

5 This major mountain range forms an arc of approximately 1,500km across Central and Eastern Europe. It is the second longest mountain range in Europe.

_____

6 This is a small landlocked country to the south of Serbia. Although the UN and EU have recognised it as an independent state, several countries including Serbia and Russia do not.

_____

Guess the Shape

Can you identify these Balkan states? Mark the location of each capital city on the map and write its name. Write the name of the country underneath each map.

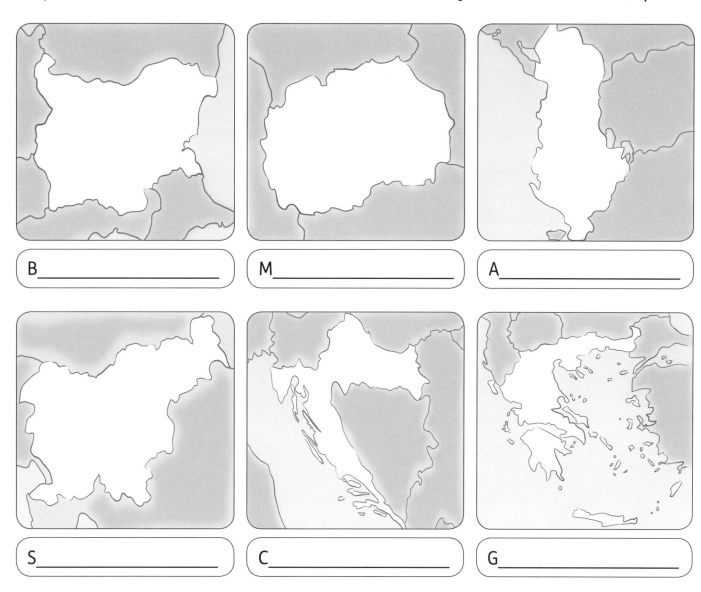

B_____

M_____

A_____

S_____

C_____

G_____

Exercise C

Pen Profile

Research the life of Mother Teresa. Find out why she was given the nickname 'the saint of the gutters'. Present your information using these headings:

- Early life
- Work in Kolkata
- What she achieved

- How she is remembered
- Irish connections

Asia

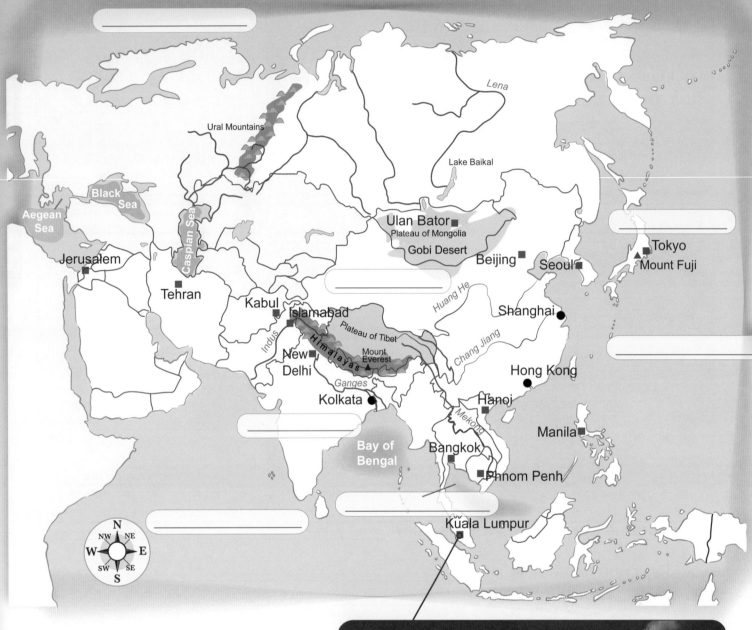

Lena

Ural Mountains

Lake Baikal

Black Sea

Aegean Sea

Jerusalem

Caspian Sea

Tehran

Kabul

Islamabad

Indus

New Delhi

Himalayas

Mount Everest

Plateau of Tibet

Ganges

Kolkata

Ulan Bator
Plateau of Mongolia
Gobi Desert

Beijing

Seoul

Tokyo
Mount Fuji

Huang He

Shanghai

Chang Jiang

Hong Kong

Hanoi

Mekong

Manila

Bangkok

Phnom Penh

Bay of Bengal

Kuala Lumpur

N
NW NE
W   E
SW SE
S

Kuala Lumpur, Malaysia

Label the seas and oceans that surround the continent of Asia.

Label Japan, India and China. Use your atlas to help you.

More about Maps!

Japan is located off the east coast of Asia. It is made up of four large islands.

The highest mountain in Japan is the snow-capped Mount Fuji.

India lies between Pakistan, Bangladesh and Nepal. Northern India is separated from the rest of Asia by the Himalayas.

Exercise A

Answer these questions:

1 What is the highest mountain in

Asia? _____

Where is it located?

_____

2 What is the longest river in Asia? _____

Describe its course. _____

_____

3 List four countries that border India and identify the capital city of each

country.

Country: _____   Capital: _____

Country: _____   Capital: _____

Country: _____   Capital: _____

Country: _____   Capital: _____

Guess What?

Tokyo is the capital city of Japan. It is one of the world's most populated cities.

There is no official religion in India. However, most people follow the Hindu religion.

4 List the countries that border Thailand and identify the capital city of each country.

Country: _____ Capital: _____

Country: _____ Capital: _____

Country: _____ Capital: _____

Country: _____ Capital: _____

5 What is the name of Japan's highest mountain?

_____

6 Name a sea that borders India.

_____

7 Where is the Gobi Desert? _____

8 Name the desert that lies to the west of India. _____

9 What is the longest river in India? _____

Exercise B

Alphabet Quiz

Work in pairs. Some of the answers can be found in this chapter. Other questions are more difficult and you will need to research the answers. Working with your partner, see how many questions you can answer now. Discuss how you will find the answers to the other questions.

What **A** _____ is the country where Kabul is the capital city?

What **B** _____ is the capital city of China?

What **C** _____ is the largest lake in the world?

What **D** _____ is a city south of the Persian Gulf?

What **E** _____ is the world's highest mountain?

What **F** _____ is the highest mountain in Japan?

What **G** _____ is the longest river in India?

What **H** _____ is an island in Japan?

What **I** _____ is an island country in Southeast Asia?

What **J** _____ is a holy city in Israel?

What **K** _____ is a country bordering Russia?

What **L** _____ is a country west of Vietnam?

What **M** _____ is a country where the Gobi Desert is located?

What **N** _____ is a country in the northeast of Asia that borders China?

What **O** _____ is a river in northern Asia?

What **P** _____ is the ocean lying to the east of Asia?

What **Q** _____ is a small country in the Middle East of Asia?

What **R** _____ is the sea bordering Saudi Arabia on the west coast?

What **S** _____ is a river in China?

What **T** _____ is a plateau in south central Asia?

What **U** _____ is a mountain range that forms the border between Asia and Europe?

What **V** _____ is a country in Southeast Asia?

What **W** _____ is a major city in China?

What **X** _____ is a major city in China?

What **Y** _____ is the longest river in Asia?
(Hint: It is also known as Chang Jiang.)

What **Z** _____ is a mountain range east of the Persian Gulf?

Fill in the missing words. Use the Word Box on page 133 to help you.

Asia is the largest _____ in the world. It is bordered by _____ and Africa on the west. The Pacific _____ lies to the east of the continent. Asia is divided into specific _____: Northern Asia, _____, Southern Asia, Eastern Asia, Central Asia and Southeast Asia.

Mount Everest, the highest _____ in the world, is found in Asia. It is located in the _____.

Sign pointing to the base camp of Mount Everest

The _____ Sea is the largest lake in the world. It is a very important lake for the fishing industry and it is also a major shipping route.

Lake Baikal is the _____ lake in the world. It is found in southern Siberia in _____.

The _____ desert is one of the greatest desert regions in the world. It stretches across Mongolia and China. This desert region consists of bare rock.

China, in eastern Asia, is the world's most populated country. The capital city of China is _____. The Great Wall of China is the biggest man-made structure on earth. It winds across northern China. The longest river in Asia is _____. Its source is in western China, in the Plateau of _____. It enters the sea near Shanghai.

India forms a peninsula. The capital city of India is _____.

The Himalayas are found to the north of India. The southeast of the country is bordered by the _____. Kolkata is one of the most densely populated cities in India. Mother Teresa of Kolkata was a famous _____ who worked with the poor people in the slums of Kolkata. In 1979 she received the _____ Prize for Peace. She died in 1997 having devoted her entire life to helping the poor.

Rice is a very popular food in Asia. It is grown in _____, which are flooded areas of arable land. Sushi is a _____ delicacy of rice and raw fish, dipped in vinegar and wrapped in seaweed.

Caspian	**New Delhi**	**Russia**	**deepest**	**paddy fields**
Nobel	**Middle East**	**nun**	**Bay of Bengal**	**Tibet**
Europe	**Chang Jiang**	**Gobi**	**Ocean**	**Japanese**
Himalayas	**regions**	**Beijing**	**continent**	**mountain**

Exercise C

Research Time

The River Ganges is considered sacred to the people of India. It is known as 'Mother Ganges'. It is also one of the most heavily polluted river systems in the world.

Research the River Ganges. What are the beliefs that are associated with the river?

Describe the activities that take place in the water and outline the reasons why the river has become so polluted. What steps are the local people taking to reduce this pollution?

Present your findings to the class.

Africa

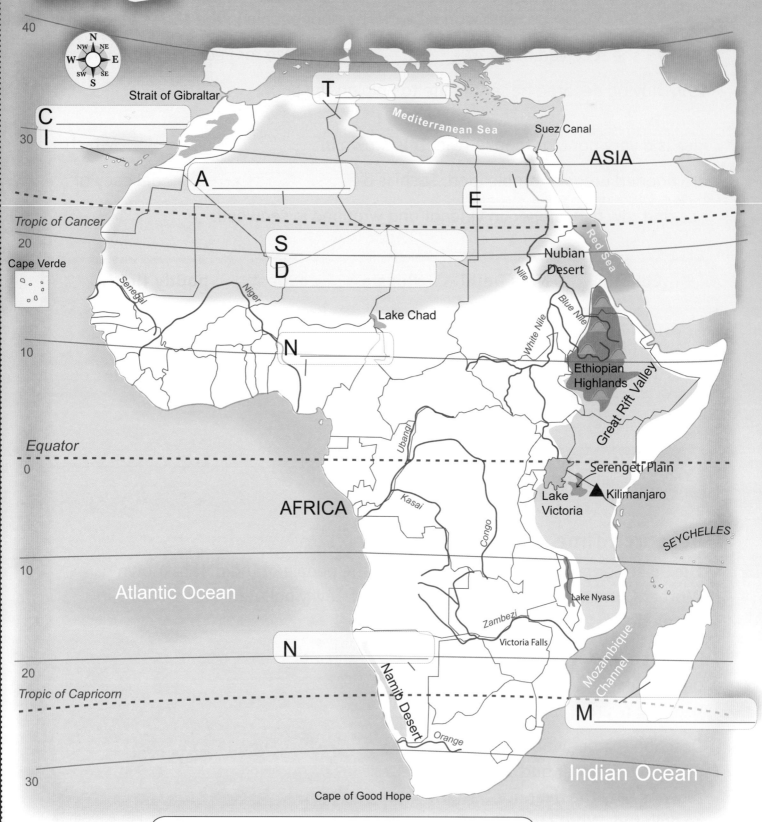

40

Strait of Gibraltar

C _____

30 **I** _____

T _____

Mediterranean Sea

Suez Canal

ASIA

A _____

E _____

Tropic of Cancer

20

Cape Verde

S _____

D _____

Nubian Desert

Red Sea

Nile

Senegal

Niger

Lake Chad

White Nile

Blue Nile

10 **N** _____

Ethiopian Highlands

Great Rift Valley

Ubangi

Equator

0

AFRICA

Kasai

Congo

Serengeti Plain

Lake Victoria

▲ Kilimanjaro

SEYCHELLES

10

Atlantic Ocean

Lake Nyasa

Zambezi

Victoria Falls

Mozambique Channel

N _____

20

Tropic of Capricorn

Namib Desert

Orange

M _____

30

Cape of Good Hope

Indian Ocean

Use your atlas to help you to fill in the missing labels on the map.

Colour three landlocked countries in Africa.

Circle the Canary Islands.

134

More about Maps!

The Suez Canal is an artificial waterway that connects the Mediterranean Sea and the Red Sea. It separates the continents of Africa and Asia. The canal reduces the journey time for ships travelling between the two continents by thousands of kilometres. Before it was opened, ships from Europe had to sail south around the Cape of Good Hope to reach Asia.

Africa is very rich in natural resources. The African economy depends heavily on the export of crops such as coffee, cacao (chocolate), peanuts and palm oil. Minerals such as gold, platinum and diamonds are also important exports.

Guess What?

The Atlas mountain range in Morocco is home to groups of African people called Berbers. Berbers have lived in Morocco for thousands of years and still follow their traditional way of life, herding sheep and goats.

Exercise A

Answer these questions:

1 What is the biggest country in Africa? _____

2 What is the biggest lake in Africa? _____

3 Name a mountain range in the northwest of Africa. _____

4 Describe the course of the River Congo. _____

_____

5 List four inland countries in Africa.

(a) _____   (b) _____

(c) _____   (d) _____

6 List four countries that share a land border with Niger.

(a) _____   (b) _____

(c) _____   (d) _____

7 Write three facts about the Sahara Desert.

(a) _____

_____

(b) _____

_____

(c) _____

_____

8 Write three facts about the River Nile.

(a) _____

_____

(b) _____

_____

(c) _____

_____

9 List some of the most important African exports.

_____

_____

_____

_____

Guess What?

Repeated natural disasters, wars and fighting mean that some of the poorest countries in the world are in Africa.

10 Why do some African countries suffer from such extreme poverty?

_____

_____

_____

_____

_____

_____

Exercise B

Fill in the missing words. Use the Word Box to help you.

The continent of Africa is the second largest continent in the world. It borders

the southern half of the _____, the _____

to the west, and the Indian Ocean to the _____.

The _____ runs from west to east, dividing the continent

into two separate halves – north and south. Some of the countries it passes

through include _____, _____,

_____ and _____. Africa also has the

longest river in the world – the _____. This flows

through several African countries, including _____ and

_____, making the land very fertile. The largest waterfall

in Africa is the _____. This is located on the border between

Zimbabwe and _____. _____ is the largest island

in the African continent, and it lies just off the east coast of Africa.

Madagascar	**southeast**	**Atlantic Ocean**	**Congo**	**Uganda**
Kenya	**Nile**	**equator**	**Mediterranean Sea**	
Sudan	**Somalia**	**Victoria Falls**	**Ethiopia**	**Zambia**

Exercise C

Dam Dilemma

The Aswan Dam took ten years to complete. Research the reasons why the
dam was opened and the benefits it has brought to Egypt. Investigate the
environmental impact of the dam. Imagine that you were a local politician
at the time. Decide whether you support or oppose the dam. Prepare a short
speech to give to your parliament, outlining your reasons.

North America

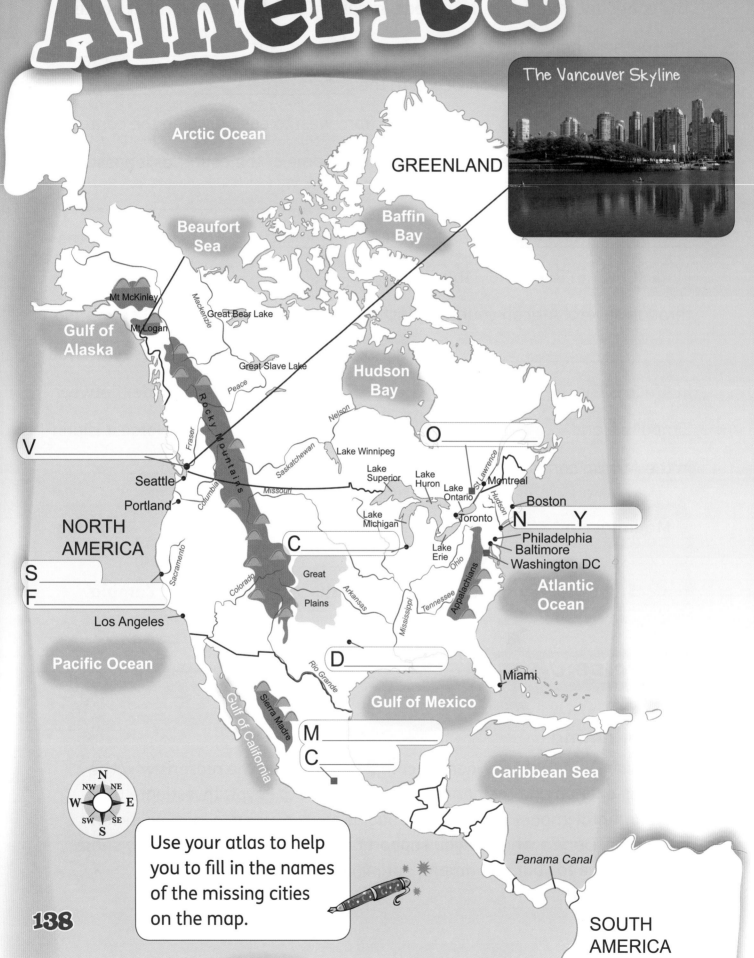

The Vancouver Skyline

Arctic Ocean

GREENLAND

Baffin Bay

Beaufort Sea

Mt McKinley

Great Bear Lake

Mackenzie

Gulf of Alaska

Mt Logan

Great Slave Lake

Peace

Hudson Bay

Rocky Mountains

Nelson

Fraser

V_____

Seattle

Lake Winnipeg

Saskatchewan

Missouri

Lake Superior

Lake Huron

St Lawrence

Montreal

O_____

Portland

Columbia

Lake Michigan

Lake Ontario

Toronto

Boston

N____ Y____

NORTH AMERICA

Sacramento

C_____

Lake Erie

Ohio

Philadelphia
Baltimore
Washington DC

S_____

F_____

Great

Plains

Arkansas

Colorado

Tennessee

Appalachians

Mississippi

Atlantic Ocean

Los Angeles

Pacific Ocean

D_____

Rio Grande

Miami

Gulf of California

Sierra Madre

Gulf of Mexico

M_____

C_____

Caribbean Sea

N
NW   NE
W   E
SW   SE
S

Use your atlas to help you to fill in the names of the missing cities on the map.

Panama Canal

138

SOUTH AMERICA

More about Maps!

North America is the third largest continent. The continent is almost completely surrounded by water – it is bordered by the Arctic, Atlantic and Pacific oceans.

The border between Canada and the United States is the longest land border in the world.

The land in the far north is icy with little vegetation. Southern areas such as Florida are lush and tropical. The snow-capped Rocky Mountains stretch from the Arctic region to New Mexico in the USA.

Greenland is the largest island in the world that is not a continent in its own right. Although Greenland is located in North America, officially it is part of Denmark.

Guess What?

The United States is one of the most developed nations in the world. It has many natural resources such as oil, gas, coal, gold, uranium and iron.

Silicon Valley is the name given to a region of northern California. This area is home to many of the world's largest computer and technology firms. The name comes from the silicon used to make computer chips.

Office building in Silicon Valley

The Statue of Liberty is one of the most well-known symbols of the United States. It stands in New York Harbour. The statue was originally given as a gift from France to the United States and was intended as a symbol of friendship and liberty.

Exercise A

Answer these questions:

1 Name the five Great Lakes.

(a) _____ (b) _____ (c) _____

(d) _____ (e) _____

2 Name two states that border the Great Lakes.

(a) _____ (b) _____

3 What American city is closest to the Arctic Circle? _____

4 Name a city in Florida. _____

5 List three American cities on the Atlantic coast.

(a) _____ (b) _____ (c) _____

6 Name two states bordering Canada.

(a) _____ (b) _____

7 Name two rivers that rise in the Rocky Mountains.

(a) _____ (b) _____

Exercise B

Write questions for these answers:

1 _____?

They are a collection of freshwater lakes located on the border between Canada and the United States. They are collectively known as the Great Lakes.

2 _____?

The region got its name from the silicon used to make computers.

3 _____?

It is known as 'the Sunshine State' because its location in southeastern USA means that it has a hot, tropical climate.

Exercise C

New York, New York!

Study the street map of Manhattan. This district is very well planned with streets and avenues. Use the map to answer the questions.

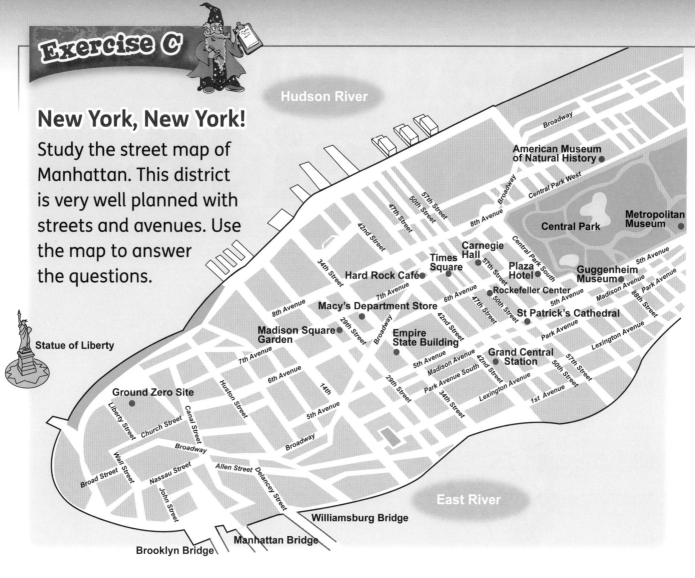

1 Name the square near Seventh Avenue and 29th Street.

_____

2 Name the building between Fifth Avenue and Madison Avenue on 50th Street. _____

3 If you were going to see a concert in Madison Square Garden, describe the route you would take from Grand Central Station. Include the names of the streets and avenues. _____

_____

4 If you were shopping in Macy's Department Store and you needed to make your way to the Guggenheim Museum, describe the route that you would take. Include the names of the streets and avenues. _____

_____

5 Imagine that you are a restaurant owner and you would like to open a new business in Manhattan. Choose a suitable location on the map for a new restaurant and give reasons for your answer. _____

_____

South America

Caribbean Sea

CENTRAL AMERICA

Panama Canal

Caracas

Orinoco

North Atlantic Ocean

Zulia

VENEZUELA

Angel Falls

GUYANA

FRENCH GUIANA

Bogota

Parima Mountains

Guiana Highlands

SURINAME

COLOMBIA

Galapagos Islands

Quito

Japura

Negro

Amazon

Equator

ECUADOR

Andes Mountains

BRAZIL

Xingu

PERU

Lima

Lake Titicaca

BOLIVIA

Brasilia

Brazilian Highlands

La Paz

Atacama Desert

PARAGUAY

Paraguay

Parana

South Pacific Ocean

CHILE

Asunción

Tropic of Capricorn

Uruguay

URUGUAY

South Atlantic Ocean

Santiago

Buenos Aires

Montevideo

ARGENTINA

Colour a country with a coastline on the South Pacific Ocean.

Colour each country that borders Brazil.

Falkland Islands

142

Cape Horn

More about Maps!

The Brazilian Highlands are an area of hills and mountains in eastern South America. They cover the eastern, southern and central parts of Brazil.

Lake Titicaca is high up in the Andes, on the border between Bolivia and Peru. It is the largest lake in South America.

 Guess What?

The Falkland Islands lie to the southeast of Argentina. The islands are a British territory and the official language is English.

In the past, ships could travel from New York to San Francisco only by sailing around Cape Horn. In 1914, the Panama Canal was opened. This has greatly reduced shipping times between the Atlantic and Pacific Oceans.

Many tribes lived in South America before the European settlers arrived. The Inca people lived in the Andes Mountains in Peru.

 **Exercise A**

Panama Canal

Answer these questions:

1 Where is the highest waterfall in the world?

_____

2 What is the smallest country in South America?

_____

3 What is the largest country in South America?

_____

4 List five countries that share a land border with Brazil.

(a) _____

(b) _____

(c) _____

(d) _____

(e) _____

5 Describe the course of the Amazon River.

_____

_____

_____

Amazon River

6 Write the names of the countries of South America that are on the Pacific Coast. Name the capital of each.

_____

_____

_____

7 Where is the source of the River Parana? _____

8 Name the sea that lies to the north of South America.

_____

9 Why was the Panama Canal constructed? _____

_____

10 Spanish and Portuguese are spoken widely throughout South America. Can you explain why this is?

_____

_____

_____

Exercise B

Write these geographical features under the correct heading:

Chile	Caribbean	Guyana	Pacific	Amazon
Atacama	Uruguay	Brazilian Highlands		Titicaca
Brazil	Argentina	Atlantic	Andes	Parana
Falklands	Negro	Xingu	Brasilia	Santiago
Buenos Aires		Montevideo	Venezuela	Peru

Ocean	
Sea	
River	
Desert	
Lake	
Mountain range	
Island	
City	
Country	

Exercise C

Inca Trail

Machu Picchu is an ancient city built by the Incas. The ruins of this magnificent city lie high in the Andes. You are a tour guide in Machu Picchu. Write an advertisement to encourage tourists to take one of your tours. Research the key sites in Machu Picchu. How will you arrange transport in and out of the city?

Machu Picchu

Australia and New Zealand

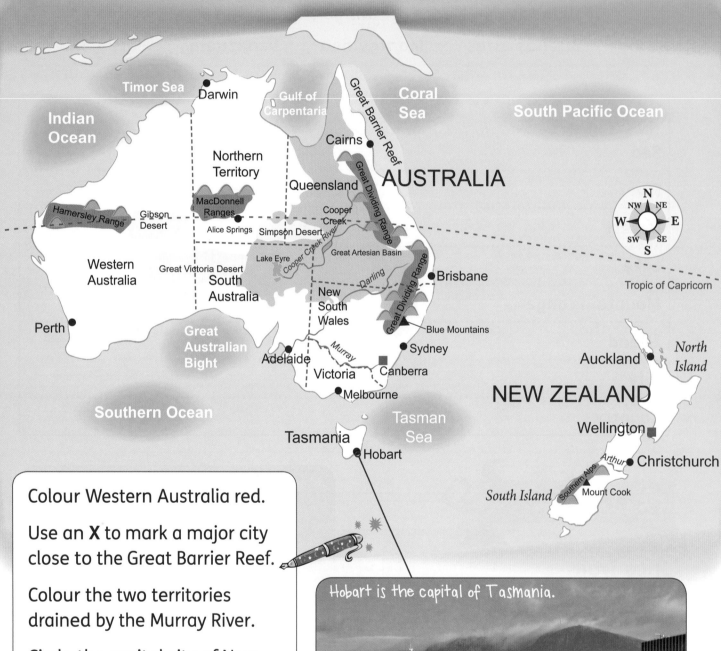

Timor Sea
Darwin
Gulf of Carpentaria
Great Barrier Reef
Coral Sea
South Pacific Ocean
Indian Ocean
Northern Territory
Cairns
AUSTRALIA
Hamersley Range
Gibson Desert
MacDonnell Ranges
Queensland
Cooper Creek
Great Dividing Range
Alice Springs
Simpson Desert
Cooper Creek River
Great Artesian Basin
Western Australia
Great Victoria Desert
South Australia
Lake Eyre
Brisbane
Tropic of Capricorn
Perth
Great Australian Bight
New South Wales
Darling
Blue Mountains
Adelaide
Murray
Sydney
Southern Ocean
Victoria
Canberra
Melbourne
Tasman Sea
Tasmania
Hobart
Auckland
North Island
NEW ZEALAND
Wellington
Arthur
Christchurch
South Island
Southern Alps
Mount Cook

Colour Western Australia red.

Use an **X** to mark a major city close to the Great Barrier Reef.

Colour the two territories drained by the Murray River.

Circle the capital city of New Zealand.

Hobart is the capital of Tasmania.

More about Maps!

The Nullarbor Plain is named after the Latin words for 'no trees'. It is a flat, treeless part of southern Australia. It is located on the Great Australian Bight coast, with the Great Victoria Desert to its north.

The Great Barrier Reef stretches along the northeast coast of Australia. This is the world's largest coral reef and is a popular tourist destination. It is home to more than 1,500 species of fish. People visit to snorkel and dive along the reef. Coral reefs are found in clear, shallow waters that have a constant warm temperature. They are very fragile and can be damaged easily by storms, changes in water temperature and pollution.

Guess What?

Most of Australia is hot, dry desert, and the country suffers badly from bushfires almost every year.

Answer these questions:

1 What is the largest lake in Australia? _____

Where is it located? _____

2 Write two facts about the Great Barrier Reef.

(a) _____

(b) _____

3 Name a desert in the northwest of Australia. _____

4 Describe the course of the Murray–Darling river system.

_____

_____

5 Describe the course of the Cooper Creek River. _____

_____

_____

6 Name the desert south of the MacDonnell Ranges. _____

7 Name the large bay shared by the Northern Territory and Queensland.

_____

8 Name the sea to the northwest of Australia. _____

9 Write two facts about the Nullarbor Plain.

(a) _____

(b) _____

Guess What?

The Sutherland Falls are found on New Zealand's South Island. They are among the highest waterfalls in the world.

Exercise B

What Am I?

1 I am a large, dry lake in the Australian outback. I am the continent's lowest point.

_____

2 I am an oval-shaped chunk of sandstone. I am the world's largest rock. I am located in the middle of the Simpson Desert. In the past, I was known as Ayers Rock. I am a sacred worship site for Aborigines.

_____

3 My name comes from the Latin words for 'no trees'. I am a flat, almost treeless area in South Australia, located on the Great Australian Bight.

_____

4 I am the biggest city in Australia. Popular tourist attractions include the famous Opera House and the magnificent Harbour Bridge.

_____

5 I take my name from Britain's Queen Victoria. With the exception of a few vehicle tracks, I am almost completely untouched by humans. I am the largest sand dune desert in Australia.

_____

6 I am the highest mountain in New Zealand. I lie in the Southern Alps, the mountain range that runs the length of the South Island.

_____

7 I am the third largest body of water in the world. I lie between Africa on the west, Australia on the east, Asia on the north, and Antarctica on the south. On St Stephen's Day 2004, a major earthquake underneath my sea bed resulted in a devastating tsunami.

_____

Down to Business

You are the owner of a scuba diving company. You organise trips to the nearby Great Barrier Reef.

Prepare a brochure for local hotels and hostels. How will you arrange transport to and from the reef? What marine wildlife will your customers see? What activities will they engage in? How will you ensure their safety? Remember that the Great Barrier Reef is extremely fragile – the local council will need to be reassured that your tour will not present any risk to the reef.

Scuba diving in the Great Barrier Reef